COMPETITIONS

maximizing your abilities

Featuring:

Academic Competitions
Fine and Performing Arts Competitions
Leadership Competitions
Service Learning Competitions

by Frances A. Karnes, Ph.D.,
and Tracy L. Riley, Ph.D.

ISBN 1-882664-28-0

For

Mary Ryan Karnes, Duncan and Shelby Riley, and to all other children
and youth who celebrate their talents through competition.

May each of you use every opportunity available
to become the best possible you!

▼ ▽ ▼ ▽ ▼ ▽ ▼ ▽ ▼ ▽ ▼ ▽ ▼ ▽

CONTENTS

▲ ◭ ◮ ▲ ◭ ▲ ▲ ◭ ▲ ▲ ◭ ▲ ▲ ◭ ▲ ◭ ▲

Sometimes a winner is just a dreamer who never gave up.
—Anonymous

Just believe in trying your best, giving full-out, and having a good attitude. If you lose, you'll have other chances.
—12-year-old girl

Competitions: What You Should Know

Have you ever created a great invention, worked on a science experiment, written an intriguing mystery, or led a service project for your community? Through competitions, you can use your skills and win in many ways. Entering competitions can be a fun and exciting part of your life!

Competition has become the backbone of our society. Adults engage in informal and formal competition nearly everyday. Yet only in the last two to three decades have competitions at the national level been available to youth. When young people participate in competitions they are preparing to be productive adults.

There are a variety of national competitions identified in this book. There likely will be several in which you'll want to be involved. You will discover great things about competitions. By participating, you will learn more about yourself and your special talents and abilities. Academic talents, such as language arts, science, mathematics, and social studies, as well as those in the fine and performing arts including drawing, painting, graphics, and photography, can be further developed. Leadership and service learning in your school and community offer special opportunities to get involved. Most competitions in this book are open to any student, but a few require membership in an organization. The competitions listed in this book may be called contests, quizzes, bowls, bees, tournaments, or be labeled with some other title. Whatever the name, you'll learn many things by competing! Whatever your interests, you'll find a competition to participate in somewhere in this book.

Who Will Benefit From This Book

This book is written for you ... elementary and secondary students. However, there are others who will also benefit from using it. Teachers will want to know the wide variety of competitions available and how to prepare their students to compete. Parents will find the number and variety of competitions of interest and will find the specifics provided helpful in assisting their children in making appropriate choices for competing. Guidance counselors and school librarians will be able to use the information to help students find appropriate outlets for their talents. Youth group directors wanting to involve students in a wide variety of positive endeavors will be helped. Share this book with teachers, parents, or other adults who can help you and your friends become involved in competitions!

How Competitions Were Selected For This Book

Those competitions for elementary and secondary students focusing on academics, fine and performing arts, leadership, and service learning were selected for inclusion in this book. Although there are many ways to compete within your community and state, we thought having information on national competitions would help you to know about many, many more in which to participate. It was important that most of those listed have no entrance fee, although a few do require a small one. Each competition sponsor had the opportunity to send us information on their event. As you read this book you will find that some provided more detailed information than others.

There are more than 100 competitions listed in this book! Much time and effort were given to locating the listed competitions. A few competitions chose not to be included or were uncertain of their funding for the future. If you know of competitions not listed here, please let us know for the next edition.

How to Use This Book

This book is divided into three sections. Part I includes more than 100 competitions in the areas of academics, fine and performing arts, leadership, and service learning. Within each of these major areas, the competitions are grouped in alphabetical order. Part II is a "Competitions Journal" which provides reproducible pages for you to record your ideas about competitions. You will have an opportunity to set goals for competition, reflect upon your feelings, and investigate new areas of interest. Part III is a resource list of books that will help you as you prepare for competitions. There are books that offer everything from how to give a speech to sharpening your skills as a photographer.

Thanks! Thanks! Thanks!

We would like to give special thanks to the individuals and groups who have been helpful in taking an idea and turning it into a book. To those adults who have conducted competitions and contributed the information on each, we owe an enormous debt of gratitude. The opportunities given to youth through each competition should be known to every student, teacher, parent, and adult working with young people, and they should avail themselves of all opportunities for participation.

We thank the many students and others who contributed their ideas on competitions through their quotations.

Barbara Harmon, Debbie Troxclair, and Kate Walker assisted with many phases of the book and we acknowledge and appreciate their suggestions and diligent efforts. For the technical preparations of the manuscript, Barbara LeSure and Shon Moss have been very helpful and patient. Jo Eidman, Trina Hira, and Kristen Stephens who served as readers for the manuscript are commended for the time and energy they spent in helping make this book one that many youth will enjoy.

We applaud Stephanie Stout, our editor, for her ideas and insights. To Joel McIntosh, our publisher, we are very grateful for his interest in our ideas and for his positive personality and futuristic thinking.

Our families are constantly helpful and supportive of our professional endeavors. Our husbands, Ray and Wade, continue to offer emotional and psychological support. Christopher, John, Leighanne, and Mary Ryan Karnes have given joy and understanding. Duncan and Shelby Riley provide encouragement and inspiration in their own special ways.

Your Benefits From Entering Competitions

There are many positive benefits from entering competitions. Here are a few:

- Competitions provide opportunities for growth and development of specific skills including:
  * creative problem solving;
  * critical thinking;
  * leadership;
  * group dynamics; and
  * communication.
- Competitions build your self–confidence, especially as you have the chance to feel a sense of satisfaction from accomplishments.
- Competitions serve as vehicles for self–directed learning which makes you more responsible in planning for and carrying out your goals.
- Some competitions offer opportunities for cooperative learning experiences when you work with teams or groups of students.
- Competitions serve as outlets for displaying a variety of great products including experiments, paintings, essays, films, inventions, photographs, songs, posters, or even sculptures.
- Competitions challenge you.
- Competitions improve your personal skills, including:
  * time management (using your time well);

* punctuality (being on time);
* following directions;
* meeting and greeting new and different people; and
* responsibility and planning.

- Competitions are a constructive use of your time. The benefits are many when you are involved in planning for and participating in competitions.
- Competitions give you a chance to experiment with some new and different "tools" for expressing yourself and your ideas.
- Competitions enhance your interests, giving you an opportunity to build on your current interests and attain new ones, too.
- Competitions give you a chance to meet many new people. Not only will you make new friends as you meet other students your age, you will meet lots of adult leaders who work in a variety of fields. Competitions serve as great networking tools.
- Competitions are a way of being recognized for your strengths, abilities, and interests.
- Finally, competitions have many other benefits. You may win awards such as scholarships; cash prizes; trophies, ribbons, and certificates; travel; or other fun prizes.

Selecting a Competition ...

As you go through this book and think about competitions that interest you, you'll have to make some decisions. Deciding which competitions best suit you is probably the most important one. Use the following steps to help you select a competition that will enhance your strengths and abilities.

- Assess your talent area. Ask yourself, "What talents do I have?" List the areas in which you do very well. Some ideas might be: math, science, history, reading, drawing, creative writing, singing, playing the piano, photography, or leadership.
- List your interests.
- List things you would like to learn more about or areas you would like to improve.
- Combine these lists. Rank order the items and select the top five areas.
- Select several competitions which may help you improve and build on your strengths and interests.
- Read the guidelines for each competition. Ask yourself the following questions:

* Can I do what is expected?
* Is this competition in my area of ability and/or interest?
* Do I have the time to participate?
* Do I have the resources for participation?
* Will I need a sponsor? If so, can I get one? How can I get one?
* If a team is needed, are there other students interested?
* Is my idea practical and original?

- Discuss your ideas with a teacher, your parents, and friends. Seek their advice. They may give you some really good ideas, but remember, they may not tell you what you want to hear. Take the suggestions that are good for you and keep working toward your goal.
- Talk to other students who have participated in the competition you selected (or one similar to it). Ask them about their experiences.
- Brainstorm and write down the positive and negative aspects of entering the competition.
- Be sure to check your calendar.
- Select a competition based upon this assessment — and have a fantastic time preparing for and participating in it.
- Evaluate yourself and the competition. Reflect on the experience, celebrate your efforts, and set new goals for future competitions.

Things to Keep in Mind About You and Competitions

Competitions and competing can have positive or other effects upon you depending on why you want to be involved. Being in a contest can help you improve and achieve, not only in the area of the competition, but also in interpersonal and personal skills. You will discover a new sense of motivation, energy, and self–confidence to improve, persevere, and excel. You will be able to gauge your own abilities against those of others. As you do so, you will find yourself working harder toward reaching your goals.

In setting your competition goals, plan to become involved only in those competitions for which you have time, abilities, and interests. Set your own priorities and stick to them. Keep yourself balanced and don't overload yourself with too many competitive events. Know when to say "no" ... for your own well–being.

Overcompetitiveness can lead to some possible pitfalls you will want to avoid. Some people may let their personal values and ethics go by the wayside and not do the right things just to become a winner. Too much rivalry may result in hurt feelings among friends. Your sense of self–worth may diminish if you don't always win, which means that your involvement in contests has gotten out of control. You may put yourself under too much pressure and set yourself up for feelings of failure. Keep your sense of humor and if you are feeling stressed out always remember that good health and exercise have been shown to help relieve stress and anxiety.

One major stress factor in becoming involved in competitions is the possibility of winning or losing. What if you don't win? Of course, you will be disappointed and unhappy. It is only natural to feel that way. But remember, competitions are learning experiences in themselves. Consider all the knowledge you'll obtain, the friends you'll make, and the opportunities you'll experience. In doing that, you will realize that just by being involved, you are already a winner.

You can also think about what you did and how you can improve. After the competition, ask yourself the following questions:

- What did I learn?
- What did I do right?
- What could I have done better?
- What do I need to do in order to do better in the future?

After examining your answers to these questions, you will want to get involved in competitions again. Feel good about yourself. Strive for improving yourself and becoming the best possible. And most importantly, remember to have fun doing it.

BE SURE TO RECORD YOUR IDEAS IN YOUR COMPETITION JOURNAL!

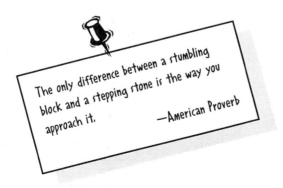

The only difference between a stumbling block and a stepping stone is the way you approach it.

—American Proverb

Members Only

There are several organizations, associations, and clubs which have competitions for members only. Usually, a membership fee and active group participation are required. You may already belong to one or more through your school or community involvement. If you would like more information, there are a couple of ways to get it. Look in your local telephone directory to see if there is a local group or ask your school counselor or principal if your school already has one. Another way to find what you need to know is to write directly to the organization. Here are some requiring you to be a member:

Boys and Girls Clubs of America
1230 W. Peachtree St.
Atlanta, GA 30309

Boy Scouts of America
1325 Walnut Hill Lane
Irving, TX 75015–2079

Business Professionals of America
5454 Cleveland Ave.
Columbus, OH 43231–4021

Cooperative Extension Service
4–H Youth Development
U.S. Department of Agriculture
Washington, DC 20250

Future Business Leaders of America
1912 Association Dr.
Reston, VA 22091

Girls Inc.
30 E. 33rd St.
New York, NY 10016

Girls Scouts of the United States of
America
830 Third Ave.
New York, NY 10022

Health Occupations Students of
America
6309 N. O'Connor Road
Suite 215LB #117
Irving, TX 75039–3510

Key Club International
3636 Woodview Trace
Indianapolis, IN 46268

National Beta Club
P.O. Box 730
Spartanburg, SC 29304

National DECA Club
1908 Association Dr.
Reston, VA 22091–1594

National Forensic League
P.O. Box 38
Ripon, WI 54971–0038

National Future Farmers of America
Organization
5632 Mt. Vernon Memorial Highway
Alexandria, VA 22309

National Junior Horticultural
Association
1424 N. 8th
Durant, OK 74701

National Scholastic Press Association
620 Rarig Center
330 21st Ave. South
Minneapolis, MN 55455–0478

Technology Student Association
1914 Association Dr.
Reston, VA 22091

United States Chess Federation
(USCF)
186 Route 9W
New Windsor, NY 12553

Vocational Industrial Clubs of
America Inc.
P.O. Box 3000
Leesburg, VA 22075

This is just a sampling of clubs and organizations which sponsor competitions. Check with your principal, teachers, or counselor to find out what else is available where you are.

Always try to do your best, no matter what anyone says, and have fun!

—12-year-old boy

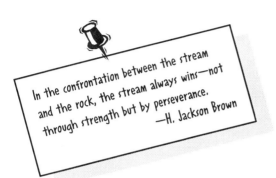

In the confrontation between the stream
and the rock, the stream always wins—not
through strength but by perseverance.
—H. Jackson Brown

ACADEMIC COMPETITIONS

Business

Competition: National Teen Business Plan Competition.

Sponsor: An Income of Her Own, P.O. Box 987, Santa Barbara, CA 93102.

Purpose: To give teens an opportunity to increase their understanding of the concepts, tools, and responsibilities of business ownership while putting their own entrepreneurial dreams on paper.

Area: Business.

Description: The competition's application provides entrants with an introduction on how to prepare a business plan and challenges them to apply and modify the basic format to fit their business idea. The message is entrepreneurs can find themselves on a path to creativity, economic security, and fun.

Eligibility: Entrants must be 13–19 years old as of the competition due date, and the competition has both male and female categories.

Guidelines Availability: Contact sponsor in April.

Deadline: See guidelines, usually in December.

Winner Notification: Winners are announced in February.

Judging Criteria: The business plan can be no longer than 10 pages and must be accompanied by the "Adult Consent" form found in the application. Entries are judged on the quality of the business plan produced, and no extra points are given for entrants who actually have a business or create the business described in the plan.

Judges: Business owners with practical experience writing and implementing business plans are judges. Judges receive a comprehensive explanation of judging criteria and a detailed scoring sheet for each plan they judge.

Awards: Winners receive a trip to a major U.S. city for the next national competition. They also receive a resource kit of products and services, and they are matched with a business owner who will act as a "Business Coach" to provide additional support and follow–up on their exploration of business and entrepreneurship.

Foreign Languages

The only people who never fail are those who never try.

—Ilka Chase

Competition: American Association of Teachers of German National Standardized Testing and Awards Program for High School Students.

Sponsor: American Association of Teachers of German Inc., 112 Haddontowne Court #104, Cherry Hill, NJ 08034–3662.

Purpose: To increase student interest in proficiency in German.

Area: German.

Description: Students are administered the American Association of Teachers of German test in their schools.

Eligibility: Open to all students of German. Those scoring at or above the 90th percentile are eligible to apply for a study trip to Germany.

Important Dates: From October to December, tests may be ordered by teachers. Testing takes place December to January.

Guidelines Availability: Write for guidelines in October.

Winner Notification: Winners are announced in April.

How to Enter: Contact the German teacher in the local high school.

Judging Criteria: Proficiency on test.

Judges: Testing Committee.

Awards: *Award I.* Students 16 years or older as of December 31 of current school year who are not graduating seniors are nominated by the Chapter Awards Committee. Applications are then forwarded to a regional selection committee. *Award II.* Graduating seniors 16 years or older as of December 31 of current school year. One student per chapter may be nominated by the Chapter Awards Committee. Applications are sent to the AATG office, and the winners are selected by a national committee. During the four weeks in Germany the students will live with German families and receive formal instruction in the German language and culture at a Gymnasium (academic high school). In addition to the national prizes, many AATG chapters have extensive awards programs of their own through which students receive cash prizes, books, pins, etc. In addition, chapters often award certificates of merit to qualifying students. Chapter Testing Committees are responsible for choosing recipients of awards, and their decisions are final.

Competition: National Greek Examination.

Sponsor: American Classical League and Junior Classical League, Department of Classics, Box 33905, University of Massachusetts, Amhearst, MA 01003–3905.

Purpose: To provide high school students of Classical and Modern Greek with an examination by which they can measure their achievement against that of students in other schools.

Areas: Greek meaning, syntax, and vocabulary.

Description: There are seven examinations in the annual battery. Each examination comprises an original Greek passage and 40 questions with multiple–choice answers on the meaning, syntax, and vocabulary of the passage. The subjects of the seven examinations are Attic Greek, levels one to three; the Iliad; the Odyssey; and Modern Greek, levels one and two.

Eligibility: High school students of Classical and Modern Greek.

Important Dates: The examination date is in mid–March.

Guidelines Availability: Year–round from sponsor.

Deadline: Early January.

Winner Notification: Upon completion of grading, typically at the end of April.

How to Enter: Contact your school guidance counselor, principal, or teacher.

Judging Criteria: Objective questions must be correctly answered.

Judges: Computer graded.

Awards: Winners of the blue, red, and green ribbons, and hand–lettered certificates are mailed to the Greek teacher at each participating school the last two weeks of April. A typed list with the names of all the winners, their ranks, and schools is mailed at the same time.

Competition: The National Junior Classical League Contests.

Sponsor: The National Junior Classical League, Miami University, Oxford, OH 45056.

Purpose: To encourage interest in the civilization, language, literature, and art of ancient Greece and Rome; to show the debt of our own civilization to that of classical antiquity.

Areas: Greek derivatives, Hellenic history/Greek literature, Latin grammar, mottoes/abbreviations and quotes, Latin derivatives, Roman history, Latin vocabulary, Roman private life and customs, Latin reading comprehension, mythology, Latin literature and academic pentathlon, dramatic interpretation, Latin oratory, English oratory, sight Latin reading, costume, slogan, essay, modern myth.

Eligibility: Secondary school students.

Important Dates: Registration requests due April 1 to May 15. Registration packets due on June 1.

Guidelines Availability: April 1-May 15.

Deadline: June 1.

Winner Notification: Prizes are presented at the convention.

How to Enter: Write for registration packet.

Judging Criteria: Varies per contest.

Judges: Selected from teachers in attendance.

Awards: Prizes awarded to the top 10 individuals in each contest; top 25 individual over-all convention winners; and top 10 individuals in each area of competition.

Competition: National Latin Exam.

Sponsor: National Latin Exam, P.O. Box 95, Mt. Vernon, VA 22121 or American Classical League, Miami University, Oxford, OH 45056.

Purpose: To promote the study of Latin.

Area: Latin.

Description: Forty multiple–choice questions include grammar, comprehension, mythology life, history, derivatives. The following exams are available: Introduction to Latin, I, II, III–IV, Prose, III–IV Poetry, and Latin V.

Eligibility: Open to all students enrolled in Latin.

Important Dates: Deadline for application is January 10. Administration takes place during the 2nd week in May.

Competition Origin: 1978.

Guidelines Availability: Ask sponsor for a copy of the syllabus.

Deadline: January 10.

Winner Notification: Mid–April.

How to Enter: Teacher sends application.

Judging Criteria: There is a percentage cutoff for various awards made by National Latin Exam.

Awards: Perfect paper certificate, gold medal and summa cum laude certificate, silver medal and maxima cum laude certificate, magna cum laude certificate, cum laude certificate, purple ribbons, *Oxford Classical Dictionaries*, and $1,000 scholarships.

Opportunity is missed by most people because it is dressed in overalls and looks like work.
—Thomas Edison

General Academics

Academic and Scholarly Recognition

Competition: Advanced Placement Scholar Awards.

Sponsor: Educational Testing Service, P.O. Box 6671, Princeton, NJ 08541.

Purpose: To recognize high school students who have demonstrated college–level achievement through AP courses and exams.

Areas: Scholar and Honor Awards across all major content areas.

Description: Students scoring 3 or higher on full–year AP examinations are honored each year at the local, state, and national level.

Eligibility: Students who have completed advanced placement courses.

Guidelines Availability: Contact school guidance counselor or sponsor.

Deadline: Contact ETS for testing schedule.

Winner Notification: Fall of each year.

How to Enter: Complete Advanced Placement examination.

Judging Criteria: Examination scores.

Judges: Educational Testing Service.

Awards: Students in the United States and Canada who receive grades of 3 or higher on three or more full–year AP examinations (or the equivalent) receive AP Scholar Awards. Students who receive grades of 3 or higher on four or more full–year AP exams (or the equivalent), with an average exam grade of 3.25, receive AP Scholar with Honor Awards. Students who receive grades of 3 or higher on five or more full–year AP examinations (or the equivalent), with an average exam grade of 3.5, receive AP Scholar with Distinction Awards. Students in schools outside of the United States and Canada who meet these criteria are awarded an International AP Certificate. The AP program recognizes the male and female high school students in each state who achieve the highest average grade on the greatest number of AP exams in their state that year. The governor of each state is invited to present these AP State Scholar Awards, and this presentation is sometimes done publicly. Finally, National AP Scholar Awards are granted to students with the highest grades on the greatest number of AP exams in the United States.

Competitions: All–USA High School Academic Team Competition.

Sponsors: USA Today, 1000 Wilson Blvd., Arlington, VA 22229–0012.

Purpose: To recognize academic excellence and leadership.

Areas: Academics and leadership.

Description: This program was designed to recognize outstanding high school students.

Eligibility: Grades 9–12.

Important Dates: Postmark nominations by late February.

Guidelines Availability: Contact the sponsor.

Deadline: Late February postmark.

Winner Notification: May.

How to Enter: Nomination forms mailed to all high school principals and guidance directors in USA and American schools overseas.

Judging Criteria: Academic excellence and demonstration of leadership are essential.

Awards: Twenty students are named to First Team and each receive a cash award of $2,500 and recognition in *USA TODAY*.

Competition: Executive Women International Scholarship Program.

Sponsor: Executive Women International, 515 S. 700 East, Suite 2E, Salt Lake City, UT 84102.

Purpose: To give scholarship awards.

Area: Academics.

Description: Scholarship monies available based upon interview and autobiographical essay.

Eligibility: Male and female high school juniors pursuing a professional area of study.

Important Dates: Competition begins in January. On May 15th district winners are announced.

Guidelines Availability: Through local chapter scholarship chair.

Deadline: Varies from chapter to chapter.

Winner Notification: Chapter EWISP chair sends notices.

How to Enter: Student needs a sponsoring teacher. Materials are distributed to local high schools.

Judging Criteria: Judging is based upon personal interviews and a student–prepared notebook which includes an autobiographical essay and lists any of the student's awards or honors.

Judges: Area individuals.

Awards: Each participating chapter gives scholarship awards of varying amounts. National awards are: 1st place — $10,000, 2nd place — $8,000, and 3rd place — $6,000. The scholarships may be used by students to attend the college or university of their choice.

Competition: Smithsonian Institution's National Summer High School Internship Program.

Sponsor: High School Internship Office, Office of Elementary and Secondary Education, A&I 2283, MRC 444 Smithsonian Institution, Washington, DC 20560.

Purpose: To select qualified candidates to participate in a six–week summer internship at the Smithsonian Institution. This educational program gives participants the opportunity to learn firsthand about a possible career while exploring the Smithsonian and nation's capital.

Areas: Biology, library science, photography, history, carpentry, education, art, computer science, and public relations (subject to change annually).

Description: Application with an essay and three letters of recommendation.

Eligibility: Graduating high school students from all social, ethnic, and cultural groups.

Important Dates: Application requests are accepted from January through the second Friday of March.

Competition Origin: 1975.

Guidelines Availability: January 1 through second Friday of March.

Deadline: Third Friday of March.

Winner Notification: First Friday of May.

How to Enter: Applications must be requested from Smithsonian between January 1 and the second Friday of March by phone or mail. The positions are designed to provide opportunities for students with a deep–seated interest in a particular field of study or career. Students can apply for only one position. Completed applications and three confidential letters of recommendation must be postmarked by the third Friday of March. Some positions have further requirements as noted in the application packet.

Judging Criteria: In this highly competitive program, acceptance is based on a demonstrated interest in a particular subject or career. Priority is given to applicants who, without financial aid, would be unable to participate. Student must be able to attend entire session.

Judges: Selection committee consists of the high school intern coordinator, assistant director of education, and two at–large members from the Smithsonian staff.

Awards: Six–week internship includes a $700 living allowance, housing in a university residence hall, and transportation arrangements to and from Washington, DC.

Advice: Request applications early. Carefully follow directions.

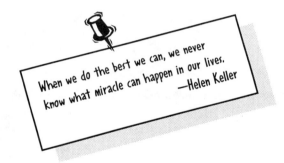

When we do the best we can, we never know what miracle can happen in our lives.
—Helen Keller

Competition: Youth for Understanding International Exchange.

Sponsor: YFU Scholarship Administration Office, 3501 Newark St. N.W., Washington, DC 20016.

Purpose: To provide scholarships for students to participate in international exchanges.

Area: Academics.

Description: Youth for Understanding International Exchange administers three scholarship programs which are funded by the governments of the United States, Finland, Germany, and Japan.

Eligibility: High school students.

Important Dates: Deadlines for applications are in late October and early November.

Guidelines Availability: Contact the sponsor in the early fall for guidelines.

Deadline: Late October and early November.

How to Enter: Students must complete application form and be nominated by a principal, teacher, or guidance counselor.

Judging Criteria: Based upon merit.

Awards: Students receive full merit–based awards to live with volunteer host families in Finland, Germany, and Japan for six weeks during the summer or during the school year.

Try it. You never know about something until you've tried it.
—13-year-old boy

Academic Quiz Bowls

Competition: Academic Games National Tournament and Academic Games Leagues.

Sponsor: Academic Games Leagues of America Inc., P.O. Box 17563 West Palm Beach, FL 33406.

Purpose: To challenge capable students in mathematics, social studies, and language arts and provide recognition for these outstanding students.

Areas: Mathematics, social studies, and language arts.

Description: Teams are composed of five players. Each player plays in a 3–person match for 30 minutes. Local league "seasons" vary from one day tournament to eight rounds over eight weeks. The national tournament takes place over four days in a different site each year.

Eligibility: Any public, private, or parochial school in the country. Participation is best through a league, but individual schools may play. Competitions conducted in four grade groups: Elementary (4–6); Middle (7–8); Junior (9–10); Senior (11–12).

Important Dates: National tournament is held in April each year. Registration deadlines begin in January.

Competition Origin: Began in 1966 in Fort Lauderdale, FL. Local leagues and national tournament have been conducted annually since then.

Winner Notification: Winners are notified at the site of each tournament.

How to Enter: Contact a local league or contact Academic Games Leagues of America Inc. at the address listed above.

Judges: Judging is conducted by local teacher/officials. Judging assistance is provided for new programs.

Awards: Local league awards are arranged from local sponsors. National tournament awards and scholarships are presented on site.

Advice: These competitions foster the same type of team camaraderie as most sports teams. Students are challenged to apply their knowledge and skills.

Competition: Knowledge Master Open (KMO).

Sponsor: Academic Hallmarks Inc., P.O. Box 998, Durango, CO 81302.

Purpose: To provide opportunities for all motivated students to participate in a national and international academic competition without the attendant expenses of traveling to a central site and to give students from schools large or tiny, urban or rural, a chance to objectively compare their achievement with thousands of the best students in top schools in the country.

Areas: All curriculum areas.

Description: The KMO is staged twice annually at both the elementary and secondary school levels. Participating teams in the KMO receive a special computer disk (Apple II, Macintosh, or IBM) with the competition questions developed especially for each meet. The teams cooperatively work to answer 200 questions at the secondary level and 100 questions at the elementary level. For each question, the team earns 5 points for a correct answer and up to 5 bonus points, depending on its speed. The secondary school competitions take about two hours, while the elementary events require about one hour. At the end of the event, team coaches call in with the number of correct answers, the number of points earned, the number of second chances answers, and a special coded score. Results are compiled the night of the competition, and all coaches are invited to phone in the morning after the event to find out their teams' ranking nationally, by state, and by enrollment division. Complete final results are mailed after the event. The various competitions attract around 5,000 schools annually and about 60,000 students. Usually all states are represented along with 10 to 20 foreign countries.

Eligibility: The KMOs are open to all students from grades 5 to 12. Each school has its own method for selecting team members. Team size is unlimited, but the average number of team members is 14.

Important Dates: The elementary KMOs are held in January and March annually. The secondary KMOs take place in December and April.

Competition Origin: The KMO was run first in 1983 and has been held twice annually ever since.

Guidelines Availability: Rules from previous competitions are available for the asking. Also, rules and suggestions are sent along with the contest kits. The kits are mailed so that materials arrive at the schools about 10 days in advance of the contest date.

Deadline: The deadlines for entering are set at two weeks before the competition dates.

Winner Notification: Winners are notified the day after the competition.

How to Enter: Academic Hallmarks publishes two free newsletters, the Knowledge Master *Aukxaminer* for elementary competitions and the Knowledge Master *Chronaukles* for the secondary competitions. These are available by writing to Academic Hallmarks. Entry forms are in these newsletters.

Judging Criteria: The KMOs are self–scoring. Winners are those teams in each of the national, state, and enrollment divisions who accumulate the greatest number of points.

Awards: More than anything else, the KMOs are nifty academic events, and most teams participate just because they are fun, challenging, educational experiences. Awards are nice trophies to the division winners and some shirts. All teams receive a poster, stickers for the individual team members, and certificates of participation. All participating schools receive a complete set of results showing the rankings of all teams in the various divisions. Many schools use this information in their accountability reports or as one of the school's quality indicators. All major national competitions which are open to only the top teams in each state accept top KMO rankings as an approved way of qualifying for those meets. A substantial number of top teams are written up in their local newspapers. Some have received congratulatory letters from the president. Others have appeared on CNN and NBC. Mostly, though, teams are involved in the KMO because it is a worthwhile educational experience in its own right, regardless of rankings.

Advice: For teams and coaches who have not participated before, it is generally a good idea to become familiar with the format of the event by working with a practice disk. The practice disks are simply the contest disks from previous years. At the end of each KMO, participants are given a special password that turns the contest disk into a practice disk. Teams will benefit by learning to communicate clearly and effectively in the context of the event and to apply various strategies for maximizing their scores.

Competition: National Academic Team Challenge.

Sponsor: Foundation for Scholastic Advancement, P.O. Box 3340, Iowa City, IA 52244–3340.

Purpose: To foster academic competition in a team setting.

Areas: English, mathematics, history, biology, chemistry, and physics.

Description: Students work together in groups of three in their own classrooms. School level winners have scores submitted for national recognition.

Eligibility: Students in grades 9 through 12.

Important Dates: Exams are held in 2 week blocks, beginning with English in mid–February, followed by history, math, biology, chemistry, and physics.

Competition Origin: 1988.

Guidelines Availability: Guidelines may be obtained by the end of September.

Deadline: End of December.

Winner Notification: Six weeks after the competition is given.

How to Enter: Write to sponsor.

Judging Criteria: Top scores are recognized.

Awards: Plaques, ribbons, and certificates.

Advice: Register early.

▼ ▽ ▼ ▽ ▼ ▽ ▼ ▽ ▼ ▽ ▼ ▽ ▼ ▽ ▼ ▽ ▼ ▽

Competition: U.S. Academic Decathlon.

Sponsor: U.S. Academic Decathlon, 11145 183rd St., Cerritos, CA 90701.

Purpose: To improve the status, the recognition, and the popularity of academic endeavor in every high school in the U.S.

Areas: Economics, essay, fine arts, interview, language and literature, math, science, social science, speech, and super quiz.

Description: The Academic Decathlon is a 10 event scholastic competition for teams of high school students.

Eligibility: Open to high school students.

Important Dates: Local competitions in November or February; National finals in April.

Competition Origin: 1982.

Guidelines Availability: Contact sponsor.

Deadline: Contact local school for try–out information.

Winner Notification: At national finals in April.

How to Enter: In many schools, try–outs for team positions occur in the fall after summer study sessions, thus involving substantially more students in the program. Local competitions are held either in November or February and in some states the local competitions in November lead to regional finals in February. The winning team from each region then advances to the state finals held each year in March.

Judging Criteria: Varies with each event.

Judges: Volunteers and company personnel.

Awards: Gold, silver, and bronze medals are awarded in each category and for each event. Overall individual winners are recognized as well as champion teams. Regional trophies were awarded for the first time in 1992. This very broad base of awards allows for major recognition of academic accomplishment.

▲ ▲ ▲ ▲ ▲ ▲ ▲ ▲ ▲ ▲ ▲ ▲ ▲ ▲ ▲ ▲ ▲

Creative Thinking and Problem Solving

Competition: Future Problem Solving Program.

Sponsor: Future Problem Solving Program, 318 W. Ann St., Ann Arbor, MI 48104–1337.

Purpose: To motivate and assist students to develop and use creative thinking skills, learn about complex issues which will shape the future, develop an active interest in the future, develop and use written and verbal communication skills, learn and utilize problem solving strategies, develop and use teamwork skills, develop and use research skills, and develop and use critical and analytical thinking skills.

Areas: The Regular Program–Group Problem Solving, The Individual Program–Individual Problem Solving, The Scenario Writing Program, and The Community Problem Solving Program.

Description: The Regular Program consists of teams of four given a futuristic "fuzzy" situation with which they must brainstorm problems, identify an underlying problem, brainstorm solutions to that problem, set criteria for judging the solutions, rank the top solutions, and pick the best solution. The Individual Program is a scaled down version of the Regular Program, consisting of just one participant. The Scenario Writing Program has participants write short stories on designated topics taking place in the future. The Community Problem Solving Programs has a team of any size identify a real life problem and follow the Regular Program steps to a best solution, and finally implement their solution.

Eligibility: The program has three levels of competition:
   a. Senior — grades 10–12;
   b. Intermediate — grades 7–9; and
   c. Junior — grades 4–6.

Important Dates: The International Conference is held during the second weekend in June.

Competition Origin: 1974.

Guidelines Availability: Contact Future Problem Solving Program.

Deadline: There is no deadline for entering into the program. However, those students who have not gone through the practice problems before attempting the qualifying problem generally do not perform as well as those who have had the experience and practice. Each state has its own deadlines for when the problems are due. For the Open Division, the qualifying problem is due by mid–March.

Winner Notification: The dates of State Bowls vary from state to state.

How to Enter: Contact Future Problem Solving Program.

Judging Criteria: For the regular and individual programs, the students are given two practice problems, which they send in. These are critiqued and returned. These are followed by the qualifying problem which qualifies them for their state bowl, or for those residing in states without affiliates, for the International Conference. Those who are invited to State Bowls are given a problem which will qualify them for an invitation to the International Conference. At the International Conference, the students are given a final problem to decide the winners in each division and category for the entire program. Top Community Problem Solving teams are invited to the International Conference to present their projects to the evaluators for final judging.

Judges: Evaluators for the International Conference are nominated by their state affiliate directors and chosen from a pool of all of those who are nominated.

Awards: The awards for winning the various competitions vary from state to state. The norm includes trophies and/or plaques. Winners at the International Conference are also awarded trophies and/or plaques.

Advice: To achieve the highest possible scores, participants are advised to utilize the practice problems, research the topic thoroughly, and keep an open mind when working on the problem for all possible solutions to their problem.

▼ ▼ ▼ ▼ ▼ ▼ ▼ ▼ ▼ ▼ ▼ ▼ ▼

Competition: Odyssey of the Mind School Program.

Sponsor: OM Association Inc., P.O. Box 547, Glassboro, NJ 08028.

Purpose: To foster creative thinking and provide creative problem–solving opportunities for all students, kindergarten through college.

Areas: Five problems are produced annually. These problems cover a variety of areas — from building mechanical devices such as spring–driven cars to presenting a creative interpretation of a literary classic.

Description: Each team performs its solution within a specified time frame and within certain cost limits. OM charters affiliates that run the local and state (association finals) competitions. These competitions culminate with an International OM World Finals competition held annually in late May or early June. Competing teams in this event represent top finishers in each U. S. state and many international counties.

Eligibility: For students in kindergarten through college. There are four divisions determined by age.

Important Dates: Local competitions begin in January and end with the OM World Finals in late May or early June. The OM membership year runs concurrent with the school year.

Competition Origin: The program began in 1978 with the first competition held in New Jersey in 1979.

Guidelines Availability: Summer of each year.

Deadline: Varies from state to state. Contact your local association director or call OM headquarters for the name of this contact.

Winner Notification: An awards ceremony follows each competition.

How to Enter: Each member is entitled to participate in the local competition. Registration varies from state to state. Contact your local association director.

Judging Criteria: There is no right or wrong answer to any problem, but there are both limitations and a specific end result that must be achieved. Teams are judged in three areas. The first is in the "long–term" problem, that is, the solution that the team has created and showcases in the competition.

▲ ▲ ▲ ▲ ▲ ▲ ▲ ▲ ▲ ▲ ▲ ▲ ▲

The second is the style. How one "markets" or elaborates the solution is considered. This may be achieved by the use of such elements as music, dance, costumes, script, etc. Finally, the spontaneous area is judged as a third category. Each team receives a problem to solve the day of the competition. The team must solve it on the spot without any preparation and within a time limit.

Judges: Judges are adult volunteers trained before the competition. Some are educators, some are business people, and others are interested parents, supporters, and former team members. The chartered associations retain the responsibility of training judges. Support materials for training are sent to each association from OM headquarters. World Finals judges must be certified.

Awards: Awards vary, but are generally medals, trophies, and certificates.

Advice: Purchase membership materials at the beginning of the school year. Local competitions begin as early as January, and students need time to develop, troubleshoot, and fine tune solutions.

One can never consent to creep when one feels an impulse to soar.

—Helen Keller

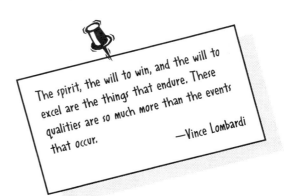

The spirit, the will to win, and the will to excel are the things that endure. These qualities are so much more than the events that occur.

—Vince Lombardi

Language Arts

Essays

Competition: Creative Writing Essay Contest.

Sponsor: Modern Woodmen of America, 1701 1st Ave., P.O. Box 2005, Rock Island, IL 61204–2005, Attn: Fraternal Department Youth Division.

Purpose: To provide students with an opportunity to demonstrate their skills in clear thinking and writing and to provide experience in an activity of value in both personal and community life.

Area: Essays.

Description: Local schools and Modern Woodmen of America representatives sponsor essay writing contest based upon a theme.

Eligibility: Students in grades 5–9.

Important Dates: Any time from September through June. The definite date will be the decision of the principal or teachers of the participating school. Please order materials one month prior to the event.

Competition Origin: January 1, 1986.

Guidelines Availability: Contact sponsor for guidelines.

Deadline: Varies with school. Check with your local sponsor.

Winner Notification: Varies with school.

How to Enter: Contact local sponsor.

Judging Criteria: Participants may receive: 20 points for creativity (presentation of idea, imagination, color, rhythm and flow, theme); 20 points for material organization (subject adherence, punctuation, grammar, vocabulary, logic, subject content); 10 points for overall effectiveness (appeal, impression, effect).

Judges: Civic leaders.

Awards: A ribbon of participation is presented to each student entering the contest as a tribute to writing ability regardless of the scoring results. Walnut and gold trophies are presented to the first, second, and third place students. A walnut and gold wall plaque is donated as a school trophy with the stipulation that the school remains in competition for five years.

Competition: Economics in One Easy Lesson Essay Contest.

Sponsor: Free Enterprise Institute, 9525 Kate Freeway, Suite 303, Houston, TX 77024–1415.

Purpose: To promote understanding of economic concepts and their application to current events, public policy issues, history, and other subjects.

Areas: Economics and essays.

Description: Students write essays that answer topical questions relating to economics.

Eligibility: Open to all high school students.

Important Dates: Guidelines are available in December.

Competition Origin: 1994.

Guidelines Availability: Obtain from sponsor in December.

Deadline: March 31.

Winner Notification: April 15.

How to Enter: Contact sponsor for contest rules, a study guide, and copies of *Economics in One Easy Lesson.*

Judging Criteria: Well–reasoned, well–written essays that answer the topical questions provided in the contest study guide.

Judges: Selected from the Free Enterprise Institute's academic advisors and staff.

Awards: $3,000 first place, $1,000 second place, and five third place $500 awards are given. The teacher who encourages each winning student will also be awarded prize money: $300 to the teacher named by the first place winner, $200 second place, and $100 each for third place winners.

▼ ▼ ▼ ▼ ▼ ▼ ▼ ▼ ▼ ▼ ▼ ▼ ▼ ▼ ▼ ▼

Competition: The Fountainhead College Scholarship Essay Contest.

Sponsor: Ayn Rand Institute, P.O. Box 6004, Inglewood, CA 90312.

Purpose: To recognize outstanding student essays.

Area: Essays.

Description: Essays will be judged on both style and content. Judges will look for writing that is clear, articulate, and logically organized. Winning essays must demonstrate an outstanding grasp of the philosophical and psychological meaning of Ayn Rand's novel *The Fountainhead*.

Eligibility: Entrant must be in the last two years of secondary school. This competition is open to all high school juniors and seniors. Scholarships are awarded on the basis of merit to outstanding essay entries.

Important Dates: Essay must be postmarked no later than April 15.

Competition Origin: The competition was begun in 1985.

Guidelines Availability: There is no deadline for guideline availability.

Deadline: All essays must be submitted by April 15.

Winner Notification: All winners will be notified by June 1.

How to Enter: Mail your essay with cover sheet.

Judging Criteria: All essays will be judged on style and content.

Judges: Essays will be selected for final judging by a national essay review board. Semi–final and finalist essays will be judged again separately.

Awards: First prize: $5,000; five second prizes: $1,000; 10 third prizes: $500.

▲ ▲ ▲ ▲ ▲ ▲ ▲ ▲ ▲ ▲ ▲ ▲ ▲ ▲ ▲ ▲

Competition: Freedoms Foundation National Awards Program.

Sponsor: Freedoms Foundation at Valley Forge, Rt. 23, Valley Forge, PA 19482–0706.

Purpose: To publicly honor and recognize the exceptional efforts of individuals, organizations, corporations, and schools who promote, through words or deeds, an understanding of responsible citizenship and the benefits of a free society.

Areas: Most youth category entries are in the form of written essays and speeches. However, projects for individual achievement or involvement in communities are also welcome.

Description: Eligible material must have been written, developed, or released during the May 1 to May 1 awards year.

Eligibility: Open to all citizens and legal residents of the U.S. grades K–12.

Important Dates: May 1 is deadline for entry. Award ceremonies are conducted by regional volunteer chapters beginning October 15.

Competition Origin: 1949.

Guidelines Availability: Year–round.

Deadline: May 1 of each year.

Winner Notification: Awardees will be announced by September 1 of each year.

How to Enter: Submit typed copy of essay or speech. Activities should be put in a ring binder or scrap book with substantiating materials.

Judging Criteria: A nomination must relate to one or more of the basic American rights set forth in the *American Credo* or the obligations outlined in the *Bill of Responsibilities*, both of which are Freedom Foundation documents available from the sponsor.

Judges: National Awards Jury is comprised of chief and associate State Supreme Court justices, executive offices from National Veteran Service and civic clubs, veterans, or educational organizations.

▼ ▼ ▼ ▼ ▼ ▼ ▼ ▼ ▼ ▼ ▼ ▼ ▼ ▼

Awards: Top recipient in Youth Category receives $100 U.S. Saving Bond and framed George Washington Honor Medal. All other recipients receive a George Washington Honor Medal.

Advice: Winning entries from other local/national contests are eligible. Entries may not be the product of classroom assignments.

Be a good winner as well as a good loser.
—14-year-old boy

▲ ▲ ▲ ▲ ▲ ▲ ▲ ▲ ▲ ▲ ▲ ▲ ▲ ▲

Competition: *Guideposts* Young Writers Contest.

Sponsor: *Guideposts* Magazine, 16 E. 34th St., New York, NY 10016.

Purpose: To promote young people's writing talent and their awareness of how faith plays a part in their everyday lives.

Area: Nonfiction writing.

Description: Students write a true personal story about an experience that deeply touched or changed their lives.

Eligibility: High school juniors and seniors, or students equivalent to those grades in other countries.

Important Dates: Entries must be postmarked by date set by sponsor in late November.

Competition Origin: 1965.

Guidelines Availability: Write sponsor.

Deadline: Entries must be postmarked with a late November date as set by sponsor.

Winner Notification: Winners are notified by mail prior to the June announcement placed in *Guideposts*.

How to Enter: Follow guidelines as described in the contest announcement.

Judging Criteria: Manuscripts must be brief — no more than 1,200 words or about five double–spaced, typed pages.

Judges: *Guideposts* staff.

Awards: First prize — $6,000 scholarship; second prize — $5,000 scholarship; third prize — $4,000 scholarship; fourth through eighth prizes — $1,000 scholarship; and ninth through 25th prizes — portable electronic typewriter. All winners receive a portable electronic typewriter and scholarships are designated for the colleges or schools of contest winners' choice.

Advice: Read contest rules carefully before submitting your story.

Competition: Letters About Literature Essay Contest.

Sponsor: *Read* Magazine, The Weekly Reader, 245 Long Hill Road, Middletown, CT 06457–9291.

Purpose: To allow students an opportunity to express their personal feelings about a book.

Areas: Essays and letter writing.

Description: Students in grades 6–10 select a book they have recently read and write a letter expressing their feelings about the book.

Eligibility: Open to all students in grades 6–10.

Important Dates: Letters are due in early December.

Guidelines Availability: Contact sponsor for a teacher's guide.

Deadline: Early December.

How to Enter: Select a book you read recently and about which you have strong feelings. You need not like the characters or even the way the events in the book turn out in order to be affected by the story. Books can make us happy, sure — but they can also frighten or anger us. Exploring why you react the way you do to literature is a valuable lesson. It teaches you about yourself. Write a letter of 1,000 words or fewer to the author, explaining what the book taught you about yourself. Make a connection between yourself and a character or an event in the book. Did you discover something you had in common with one of the characters? Did the story mirror your life in some way? What questions did the book make you ask yourself, or others?

Awards: One grand prize winner receives an all–expenses–paid trip for two to Washington, DC, to attend a special luncheon at the Library of Congress. Nine national finalists receive $100 cash awards. Participating state centers may award additional prizes.

Advice: Do not summarize the plot of the book. Why? Because the author wrote the story and already knows what happened. What the author doesn't know is the ways in which the book affected you. In other words, think of the audience to whom you are writing—the person who will read the letter. Be honest, personal, and conversational, as if the author were a friend who would write back to you.

Competition: Mothers Against Drunk Driving Annual Poster/Essay Contest.

Sponsor: Mothers Against Drunk Driving, 5111 E. John Carpenter Frwy., Suite 700, Irving, TX 75062–8187.

Purpose: To provide an excellent opportunity to express creativity and educate families and peers about the dangers of underage drinking.

Areas: Essay writing and poster design.

Description: An annual competition designed to reach current and future drivers—many of whom are directly affected by alcohol–related crashes. Students may choose to enter a poster or an essay.

Eligibility: Open to students in grades 1–12.

Guidelines Availability: The rules, entry form, and the annual theme are available in the early fall each year.

Deadline: Each year the MADD National Office sets and announces a national entry deadline. All entries from first place winners in local or statewide contests and from those entering the "Individual Competition" must be postmarked by that date and mailed to the MADD National Office.

Winner Notification: The national winners are notified by telephone and letter within one week of judging.

How to Enter: Obtain entry form from local MADD chapters or by calling or writing to the MADD National Office.

Judging Criteria: Originality, uniqueness, reflection of creative thinking, style, expression, spelling, neatness, legibility, degree of mental impact, and appropriateness and relationship to contest theme.

Judges: Judges are chosen who have qualifications in education,art, writing, design, substance abuse prevention, traffic safety, etc.

Awards: Prizes vary from year to year.

Competition: National Americanism Essay Contest.

Sponsor: AMVETS and AMVETS Auxiliary; Program National Headquarters, 4647 Forbes Blvd., Lanham, MD 20706–4380.

Purpose: To promote Americanism through essay writing.

Area: Essay writing.

Description: All essays must be written in ink in the students' own handwriting. All students must address the theme which changes annually. See contest flyer or contact your local AMVETS post. Sixth grade students should submit essays with 250 words or fewer. Ninth grade students should submit essays of 350 words or fewer. Eleventh and 12th grade students should submit essays of 500 words or fewer.

Eligibility: All students in the sixth, ninth, 11th and 12th grades who are attending public, private, or parochial schools are eligible to enter.

Important Dates: National deadline is July 1.

Guidelines Availability: Contact sponsor.

Deadline: July 1 is the deadline for national competition. Local and state deadlines may vary.

How to Enter: Application is available from the sponsor.

Awards: First place — $1,000 scholarship and plaque; second place — $750 scholarship; and third place — $500 scholarship.

Competition: National Council of Teachers of English Achievement Awards in Writing.

Sponsor: National Council of Teachers of English, 1111 W. Kenyon Road, Urbana, IL 61801-1096.

Purpose: To assist students planning to pursue degrees in English to successfully enter college.

Area: Writing.

Description: Students submit two pieces of original writing. The first is an impromptu essay and the second is a best writing sample which may consist of a poem or short story.

Eligibility: Open to all students in 11th grade.

Important Dates: Deadline for nominations by teachers is January 23. Topics are mailed out in March with entries sent to state coordinators in April. In August state coordinators mail results to NCTE. Winners are announced in October.

Competition Origin: 1957.

Guidelines Availability: Contact office for a brochure.

Winner Notification: Announced in October.

How to Enter: Students must be nominated by their English teachers.

Judges: Each state coordinator selects judges who may be English teachers, college professors, or other professionals in English.

Awards: Each winner receives a certificate, booklet, letter, and scholastic form. Cards stating that they are winners are also sent and can be attached to college applications in order to assist with financial needs or college entry.

Advice: Tenth graders with outstanding writing skills should contact the 11th grade English teacher now.

Competition: National Peace Essay Contest.

Sponsor: United States Institute of Peace, 1550 M St. N.W., Suite 700, Washington, DC 20005.

Purpose: To promote serious discussion among high school students, teachers, and national leaders about international peace and conflict resolution, complement existing curricula; and strengthen students' research, writing, and reasoning skills.

Areas: Writing and civic education.

Description: Students write an essay on the chosen topic which may focus on topics such as international affairs, conflict resolution, social studies, history, or politics.

Eligibility: Open to U.S. citizens in grades 9-12, including those attending a high school correspondence program or an American school overseas.

Important Dates: The deadline for entry is early February.

Competition Origin: In the belief that questions about peace, justice, freedom, and security are vital to civic education, the competition was established to expand educational opportunities.

Guidelines Availability: Contact the sponsor in the fall.

Deadline: Early February.

Winner Notification: Winners are notified in May.

How to Enter: Students submit a 1,500 word essay on the chosen topic. Three copies are sent to the sponsor with an application form.

Judging Criteria: Each aspect of the given topic must be addressed. Entries are judged for their research, analysis, and form.

Awards: One winner from each state receives a $750 scholarship and a trip to Washington, DC. These winners compete for national prizes of $5,000, $2,500, and $1,000.

Competition: National Society Daughters of the American Revolution Good Citizens Contest.

Sponsor: National Society Daughters of the American Revolution, 1776 D St. N.W., Washington, DC 20006–5392.

Purpose: To encourage and reward the qualities of good citizenship.

Area: Citizenship.

Description: The DAR Good Citizens Scholarship Contest consists of two parts. Part I (Personal) is a series of questions asking the student to describe how he or she has tried to manifest the qualities of a Good Citizen. This part may be completed at home and is to be submitted together with a copy of his or her scholastic record and one letter of recommendation. Part II (Essay) is to be administered under the supervision of faculty or DAR member. It must be completed at one sitting, within a two–hour time limit, and without assistance or reference materials. Part I and Part II each represent half of the total contest entry score. Each contest entry is evaluated by independent judges with the first place entry automatically forwarded on to the next level of judging until, ultimately, the final entries are judged on the national level and the national winners are selected.

Eligibility: Both males and females may enter. Program is open to all senior class students enrolled in accredited public or private secondary schools or secondary schools which are in good standing with their state board of education. U.S. citizenship is not a requirement.

Important Dates: DAR national vice chairmen shall have state winner contest entries judged and all first place division winner entries should be sent to national chairman by mid–February.

Competition Origin: 1934.

Guidelines Availability: Information can be obtained through the DAR state chairman in your state.

Deadline: Mid–February.

Winner Notification: Winners are notified by March 10th.

How to Enter: Contact DAR Good Citizen State Chairman of the state in which student resides.

Judging Criteria: Must have qualities of dependability, service, leadership, and patriotism.

Judges: The State Society DAR and the State Department of Education determine the method of selection of the State DAR Good Citizen. School DAR Good Citizen: Each school chooses its own student for this honor.

Awards: The national awards are as follows: First place winner: $5,000 scholarship; second place winner: $2,000; third place winner, $1,000. Each state and division winner receives $250.

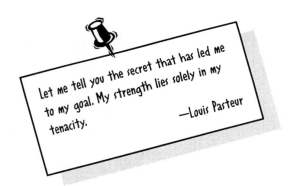

Let me tell you the secret that has led me to my goal. My strength lies solely in my tenacity.

—Louis Pasteur

Competition: National Women's Hall of Fame Poster and Essay Contest.

Sponsor: National Women's Hall of Fame, P.O. Box 335, 76 Fall St., Seneca Falls, NY 13148.

Purpose: To honor women whose contributions to American society have been of great value to our country.

Areas: Essays and posters.

Description: All entries must have a cover page. Name, school, home and school addresses, and grade level of the author must appear on the cover page. Also, please attach a copy of the official entry form to each entry as a cover sheet. Entries will be disqualified if these criteria are not met.

Eligibility:
Intermediate School: Open to all students enrolled in grades 4, 5, and 6. Essays should be 200 words, hand–written, one side only, skipping every other line.
Middle School: Open to all students enrolled in grades 7, 8, and 9. Essays should be 300–400 words, typed, and double-spaced.
Senior High: Open to all students enrolled in grades 10, 11, and 12. Essays should be 400–500 words, typed, and double-spaced.

Important Dates: Deadline for entry is March 31.

Guidelines Availability: Ongoing availability from the sponsor.

Deadline: March 31.

Winner Notification: May.

How to Enter: Write for guidelines.

Judging Criteria: The essays are judged holistically within grade groups with attention given to: adherence to topic, accuracy of facts (correct historical data), mechanics (correct spelling and grammar), creativity and originality, organization, and correct length.

Awards: The top three entrants in each essay level receive a Certificate of Achievement and cash prizes. The first prize winner receives $100; the second prize winner receives $75; and the third prize winner receives $50.

Competition: Olympic Size Morgan Horse Dreams.

Sponsor: The American Morgan Horse Association, P.O. Box 960, Shelburne, VT 05482–0960.

Purpose: To provide students an opportunity to describe in their own words their "Olympic Size Morgan Horse Dreams."

Areas: Essays and poetry.

Description: Students write an essay of 1,000 words or less or a poem on the topic "Olympic Size Morgan Horse Dreams." Students are asked to write about what this statement means to them.

Eligibility: Participants must not have reached their 22nd birthday as of December 1.

Important Dates: December 1 postmark for essays or poems submitted.

Guidelines Availability: Contact sponsor in early fall.

Deadline: December 1 postmark for essays or poems submitted.

Winner Notification: Upon completion of judging.

How to Enter: The entry form must be attached to your work in order to be considered in the contest.

Judging Criteria: Essays and poetry will be judged on general style, originality, grammar, spelling, and punctuation. The judge's decision will be final.

Judges: American Morgan Horse Association officials.

Awards: Cash awards of $25 will be presented to the winner in both categories: Essay and Poetry. Ribbons will be awarded to the first through fifth place winners in each category.

Advice: Entries will not be returned. Work submitted may be used for promotional purposes by AMHA. Students may see poems or essays in *The Morgan Horse* magazine or on the youth pages in the *AMHA News* and *Morgan Sales Network*.

Competition: PROJECT: Learn MS Scholarship Essay Competition.

Sponsor: Multiple Sclerosis Association of America, 601 White Horse Pike, Oaklyn, NJ 08107.

Purpose: To provide students an opportunity to learn about the most prevalent neurological disease affecting young adults in the U.S. and to become aware of the special needs of the disabled community.

Area: Essays.

Description: High school students submit essays on the topic of multiple sclerosis.

Eligibility: High school sophomore, junior, or senior.

Important Dates: Entries must be submitted by mid– to late–May.

Guidelines Availability: Contact sponsor.

Deadline: Mid– to late–May is deadline for submission.

Winner Notification: By early summer winners are notified.

How to Enter: Write 300–500 words; collect sponsorship; complete registration form; collect monies; and submit entry to sponsor.

Judging Criteria: Originality, content, grammar, and style.

Judges: MSAA selected judges.

Awards: Scholarship awards for top writers: one Golden Scholarship — $7,000 scholarship to the college of choice, nine Silver Scholarships — $1,000 scholarships to the college of choice.
For those students who also raise money For MS:
    Three Grand Prize winners will receive a 13–inch color Zenith TV remote for raising the most funds (minimum $250 raised).
    Raise $90 or more and receive a special design PROJECT: Learn MS Sweatshirt.
    Raise $45 and receive a special design PROJECT: Learn MS T– Shirt.

▽ ▽ ▽ ▽ ▽ ▽ ▽ ▽ ▽ ▽ ▽ ▽ ▽ ▽

Competition: Promising Young Writers Program.

Sponsor: National Council of Teachers of English, 1111 W. Kenyon Road, Urbana, IL 61801–1096.

Purpose: To develop skills in writing.

Areas: Poetry, prose, and essays.

Description: Each participant must submit a "Best Writing Sample" which may be poetry or prose. They must also write on an "Impromptu Theme," developed by the Promising Young Writers Advisory Committee.

Eligibility: Only students who are eighth graders in the current academic school year are eligible to be nominated for the Promising Young Writers program. The number of nominees allowed from each school is determined by its eighth grade average daily enrollment.

Important Dates: January 20 is deadline for nomination.

Competition Origin: 1984.

Guidelines Availability: From the sponsor in the early fall.

Deadline: Entries and fees must be received by January 20.

Winner Notification: All certificates will be mailed to school principals, who will be asked to present them to each student who submitted writing samples. Nominating teachers will also be notified.

How to Enter: Complete a nomination form for each student nominee.

Judging Criteria: Papers will be judged on content, purpose, audience, tone, word choice, organization, development, and style. Judges take into account that the writers are eighth grade students, not professional writers, and that the impromptu papers are written under time constraints.

Judges: Teams of teachers at the state level will judge the writing and select Promising Young Writers.

Awards: Each student who enters and writes will receive a citation. Certificates of Recognition will be awarded to students cited as winners. Certificates of Participation will be awarded to other nominees who write.

△ ▲ △ ▲ △ ▲ △ ▲ △ ▲ △ ▲ △ ▲ △ ▲

Competition: RespecTeen Letter–Writing Contest.

Sponsor: Speak for Yourself Lutheran Brotherhood, 625 Fourth Ave. South, Minneapolis, MN 55415.

Purpose: To encourage students to identify, reflect upon, and act upon issues affecting their lives; to foster communication about youth issues within students' families; and to help students understand how government introduces and passes laws and makes policy decisions.

Areas: Social studies, government, and history.

Description: Students participate in an activity in which letters are written to U.S. representatives about a youth issue, suggesting an approach or solution. One student from each state is invited to a Youth Forum in Washington, DC.

Eligibility: Open to all students in grades 7 and 8.

Competition Origin: 1989.

Guidelines Availability: Write to the sponsor for guidelines. A videotape is also available for preview.

Deadline: January 31 postmark.

How to Enter: Each student must write a letter to the U.S. representative from his or her district discussing an issue affecting young people on a national level and suggesting a solution. The body of the letter should be between 150 and 300 words in length and a standard format must be followed.

Judging Criteria: Issues must be based upon fact. Entries are judged based upon quality and clarity of thought, argument, supporting data, and expression, as well as sincerity and originality. All entries must be in English and those that are not legible will be disqualified.

Judges: Appointed by RespecTeen.

Awards: At the congressional district level, each winner receives a certificate, $50 U.S. Savings Bond, and pending the consent of the representative, personal congratulations from his or her U.S. Representative. At the state level, each winner receives a trip to Washington, DC, including airline tickets, food, and lodging. Each student winner and one parent/guardian participates in the RespecTeen National Youth Forum held in April.

Competition: UNA–USA National High School Essay Contest on the United Nations.

Sponsor: United Nations Association of the United States of America, 485 Fifth Ave., New York, NY 10017.

Purpose: To engage students in grades 9–12 nationwide in a serious research and writing exercise about the United Nations and the issues confronting the world organization and to broaden the perspectives of American students to better understand the complexities of our world and the challenges our nation faces as a member of the international community.

Area: Global issues.

Description: High school students write and submit essays on the United Nations.

Eligibility: Open to all students in grades 9–12.

Important Dates: The topic for the contest is announced and distributed to participating chapters, divisions, and affiliated organizations of UNA–USA in September. UNA–USA staff produces promotional materials and information about the contest that is distributed to participating groups in the contest. Participating chapters, divisions, and affiliated organizations of UNA–USA organize and conduct local contests for high school students in their area. Deadline for students submitting essays to participating chapters, divisions, and affiliated organizations is March 1. The national competition among the top essays submitted from each local contest is conducted in April. The finalists are judged in the latter part of April. The three national prize–winning essays are announced in May.

Competition Origin: 1985.

Guidelines Availability: Obtain from sponsor in September.

Deadline: March 1.

Winner Notification: May.

How to Enter: To enter the program, teachers and students are encouraged to contact their local United Nations Association chapter or the sponsor.

Judging Criteria: Decisions based upon research and writing, as well as demonstration of an understanding of the issue.

Judges: National panel of experts.

Awards: Three awards are given annually: cash awards of $1,000 (first prize), $750 (second prize), and $500 (third prize) and an all–expenses–paid trip for the prize–winning students and their teachers to New York City for the awards ceremony.

In great attempts it is glorious even to fail.
—Vince Lombardi

▼ ▼ ▼ ▼ ▼ ▼ ▼ ▼ ▼ ▼ ▼ ▼ ▼ ▼

Competition: United Nations Pilgrimage for Youth.

Sponsor: The Odd Fellows and Rebekahs, P.O. Box 1778, Palm Harbor, FL 34682–1778.

Purpose: To study and learn about the United Nations.

Area: Global issues.

Description: Students complete a U.N. exam, submit an essay, and/or participate in a speech contest. Selected winners receive an expenses–paid trip to New York City.

Eligibility: Open to students ages 16–17.

Important Dates: Dates vary. Make application for more information.

Competition Origin: June 1950.

Guidelines Availability: Contact local Odd Fellow and/or Rebekah Lodges.

Winner Notification: Prior to June trip.

How to Enter: Contact local Odd Fellow and/or Rebekah Lodges.

Judging Criteria: Applications are reviewed by selecting committees for evidence of scholarship, leadership, character, extra–curricular activities, concern for community welfare, interest in world affairs, and general fitness to participate in the program.

Awards: Each year, during June and July, North American students travel by bus to and from New York City, visiting monuments and places of interest on the way. The Odd Fellows and Rebekahs sponsor the entire cost of the tour. They are housed four to a room in New York, sharing with students from as far away as Australia, Denmark, Finland, Germany, Norway, Sweden, and Switzerland. The week–long schedule includes four half day visits to the United Nations where students are allowed to listen to behind–the–scenes briefings on specialized U.N. agencies and departments, witness a council or committee in action, see business conducted in the six official languages of the U.N., and take a guided tour.

Advice: Students who are interested should contact their local Odd Fellow and/or Rebekah Lodges.

▲ ▲ ▲ ▲ ▲ ▲ ▲ ▲ ▲ ▲ ▲ ▲ ▲ ▲

Competition: Voice of Democracy Audio Essay Scholarship Competition.

Sponsor: The Veterans of Foreign Wars of the United States and its Ladies Auxiliary, VFW Building, 406 W. 34th St., Kansas City, MO 06411.

Purpose: To allow students the opportunity to voice opinions on a patriotic theme.

Area: Essays.

Description: High school students compete for prizes and money with winners selected based upon an audio essay. This is an essay recorded on a cassette tape as read by the student.

Eligibility: All 10th, 11th, and 12th grade students.

Important Dates: Entry deadline is November 15.

Competition Origin: 1946.

Guidelines Availability: Contact local VFW Post or Auxiliary in May.

Deadline: Entry deadline is November 15. National deadline is January 15.

Winner Notification: Announced in March at the annual Veterans of Foreign Wars Washington Conference.

How to Enter: Contact sponsor for official rules.

Judging Criteria: Originality, content, and delivery.

Judges: Selected by VFW, including representatives from the major broadcast networks and government officials.

Awards: Each state winner receives a five–day all–expenses–paid trip to Washington, DC, plus the opportunity to compete for national scholarships totaling more than $100,000. National awards include: first place—$20,000; second place—$15,000; third place—$10,000; fourth place—$6,000; fifth place—$5,000; sixth place—$4,000; seventh place—$3,000; eighth place—$2,500; ninth place—$2,000; 10th through 16th places—$1,500; all additional scholarships—$1,000.

Advice: Carefully read guidelines for details.

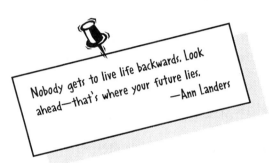

Nobody gets to live life backwards. Look ahead—that's where your future lies.
—Ann Landers

General Language Arts

▼ ▽ ▼ ▽ ▼ ▽ ▼ ▽ ▼ ▽ ▼ ▽ ▼ ▽ ▼ ▽ ▼ ▽

Competition: Cricket League.

Sponsor: The *Cricket* Magazine Group, 315 Fifth St., P.O. Box 300, Peru, IL, 61354–0300.

Purpose: To encourage readers' literary and artistic creativity and to provide a forum for personal expression.

Areas: Stories, poetry, art, or photography.

Description: Topics are drawn from issues of *Cricket* Magazine. Poems must be 24 lines or fewer, stories must be 350 words or fewer. All work must be original, without help from anyone.

Eligibility: Readers of any age or gender may enter.

Competition Origin: It began with the September 1973 launch of *Cricket*, a literary magazine for readers ages 9 and up.

Guidelines Availability: Stated on page 61 of each issue of the magazine.

Deadline: For each month's contest, entries must be received by the 25th of that month.

Winner Notification: Approximately one month after entry deadline.

How to Enter: Entries should be mailed to Cricket League.

Judging Criteria: Stories, poems, art, and photography are judged for their technique, originality, and adherence to contest themes and guidelines.

Judges: Members of *Cricket*'s editorial and art departments.

Awards: Eight to 15 winning entries (depending on space available) are published in two age categories (10 and under, and 11 and up) available in the issue three months after the issue in which the contest description appeared.

▲ ▲ ▲ ▲ ▲ ▲ ▲ ▲ ▲ ▲ ▲ ▲ ▲ ▲ ▲ ▲ ▲ ▲

Competition: *Merlyn's Pen: The National Magazine of Student Writing.*

Sponsor: Merlyn's Pen Inc., P.O. Box 910, East Greenwich, RI 02818.

Purpose: To broaden and reward the young author's interest in writing and promote among all students a positive attitude toward literature.

Areas: Short stories, poems, essays, reviews, letters, plays, and artwork of all types.

Description: Students submit their writing or artwork to *Merlyn's Pen*. It is judged for publication purposes. Once it is accepted it is published in the quarterly magazine.

Eligibility: All students in grades 6 through 12.

Important Dates: Continuous submission policies eliminate final deadlines, entrance cut–offs, etc.

Competition Origin: 1985.

Guidelines Availability: Contact *Merlyn's Pen*, or you may find them in the magazine, available in bookstores or by subscription.

Deadline: Submissions are accepted throughout the year.

Winner Notification: A decision letter and comments on each manuscript are sent within 10 weeks.

How to Enter: Students follow submission guidelines to submit their writing and artwork with a cover sheet and a submission postage/handling fee.

Judging Criteria: Manuscripts are evaluated for reader interest, authenticity of voice, mind, and the clear expression of young adult authors.

Judges: Judges are editors, who are also teachers, writers, and artists from around the country.

Awards: Publication in either the Middle School Edition or Senior Edition Magazine's quarterly publication.

▼ ▼ ▼ ▼ ▼ ▼ ▼ ▼ ▼ ▼ ▼ ▼

Competition: National Language Arts Olympiad.

Sponsor: National Language Arts Olympiad, Box 2196, St. James, NY 11780.

Purpose: To improve language arts skills.

Areas: All areas of language arts.

Description: Students take 50–question tests in the area of language arts.

Eligibility: Open to students in grades 2–12.

Important Dates: Register by February 10.

Competition Origin: 1982.

Guidelines Availability: Available in May of each year.

Winner Notification: May.

How to Enter: Register by mail to the sponsor.

Judging Criteria: Varies with each area of competition.

Awards: Medals and certificates are given to high scorers.

▲ ▲ ▲ ▲ ▲ ▲ ▲ ▲ ▲ ▲ ▲ ▲ ▲

Competition: National Writing and Art Contest on the Holocaust.

Sponsor: The United States Holocaust Memorial Museum, 100 Raoul Wallenberg Place, S.W., Washington, DC 20024–2150, Attention: National Writing and Art Contest.

Purpose: To invite students to reflect on a topic relating to the Holocaust and to think about its implication to their lives today.

Areas: Writing and art.

Description: Students should submit poems, newspaper articles, stories, plays, essays, and research papers.

Eligibility: Open to all students in grades 7–12.

Important Dates: The deadline changes each year. However, it is generally the first week in April.

Competition Origin: The museum has sponsored a National Writing Contest for 10 years and an Art Contest for 2 years.

Guidelines Availability: Contact the sponsor.

Deadline: Changes each year.

Winner Notification: Winners are notified at the end of May, and the awards ceremony for the winners is in July.

How to Enter: The guidelines for the National Writing and Art Contest are available during the first week of January each year. Teachers should write or call to receive the brochure which includes all information necessary to enter the contest. The topic changes each year so it is important to have the brochure for the current year.

Judging Criteria: Judges look for originality, content, quality of expression, and historical accuracy.

Judges: Museum staff act as the preliminary judges for the contests. After the entries are narrowed down to 25 in each category, they are sent to the "official judges." The "official judges" are made up of survivors, historians, artists, writers, museum professionals, and educators throughout the United States who volunteer to judge the contests.

Awards: First place winners are flown to Washington, DC, to visit the United States Holocaust Memorial Museum for a special ceremony. Second place winners receive a framed reproduction of artwork from the United States Holocaust Memorial Museum collection and all winners and their school libraries receive sets of books about the Holocaust and certificates of appreciation. There are prizes for first, second, and third place winners, and two honorable mentions.

Advice: Written entries should not be sent with report covers or decorative cover pages.

Competition: Reflections Cultural Arts Program.

Sponsor: The National PTA, 330 N. Wabash Ave., Suite 2100, Chicago, IL 60611–3690.

Purpose: To provide opportunities for students in preschool through the 12th grade to express and share their creative abilities. Each year works of art are inspired by a theme which is chosen from hundreds of student theme entries.

Areas:

Arts Areas	Grade Divisions
Literature	Primary preschool–2
Music	Intermediate 3–5
Photography	Middle/Junior 6–8
Visual Arts	Senior 9–12

Description: This competition is designed to give preschool through high school students opportunities to express and share their creations.

Eligibility: Any PTA/PTSA in good standing may sponsor the Reflections Program. Students must participate in Reflections through their local PTA/PTSA. The National PTA does not limit the number of entries a student may submit. Local and state PTAs may set limitations at their discretion.

Important Dates: Contact state PTA for dates.

Guidelines Availability: Available from state PTA.

Deadline: Varies for each state. Contact state PTA for dates.

Winner Notification: Each state president receives a list in May. All participants receive a certificate and letter of congratulations or regret at this time.

How to Enter: State PTAs submit entries to national level.

Awards: The National PTA awards first, second, and third place in each arts area, in each grade division. Honorable mentions may be chosen in each art category and grade division. Place winners receive a cash prize ($300, $200, or $100), a certificate, and a book is donated to each of their schools. One outstanding interpretation winner is chosen from the place winners in each arts area (a total of four). These winners receive an expenses–paid trip to the National PTA convention with one adult, a $250 scholarship, and a gold–plated Reflections medallion.

Advice: Each entry must be the work of one student. Each student and his or her parent or guardian must sign the affirmation sentence on the official entry form stating that the entry is original. Artwork may be created in or outside of school.

If you don't qualify or win, don't worry about it. It's the learning experience that counts the most. Besides, you can always try again!

—12-year-old girl

Competition: Reflections Scholarship Competition.

Sponsor: The National PTA, 330 N. Wabash Ave., Suite 2100, Chicago, IL 60611–3690.

Purpose: To provide scholarships for students wishing to pursue arts in their future education.

Areas: Literature, music, photography, and visual arts.

Description: The Reflections Scholarship Competition consists of four scholarships of $750 each, one in each of four arts areas: literature, music, photography, and visual arts. It is directed toward students who wish to pursue the arts in their future education.

Eligibility: Each student must be a senior in high school.

Important Dates: Deadline for requesting application is last Friday in November.

Guidelines Availability: Contact sponsor.

Deadline: The deadline for requesting an application is the last Friday in November. After that date, applications may be requested from your state PTA office. All requests must include the national ID number for your local PTA unit which can be acquired through your local unit president or state office.

Winner Notification: Announced in March.

How to Enter: Submit two original works.
Submit a completed application packet including:
- a personal essay;
- completed entry forms (with signed verification from the local PTA president and national ID number for the local PTA unit); and
- teacher's letter of recommendation (including recommendation form).

Judging Criteria: Judging criteria include maturity of work, articulation of personal goals in the essay, and teacher's letter of recommendation.

Judges: A jury is assembled from professionals from each arts area.

Awards: Four scholarships of $750 each.

▼ ▾ ▼ ▾ ▼ ▾ ▼ ▾ ▼ ▾ ▼ ▾ ▼ ▾ ▼ ▾ ▼

Competition: *Read* Writing and Art Awards.

Sponsor: *Read* Magazine, Weekly Reader Corp., 245 Long Hill Road, Middletown, CT 06457.

Purpose: To encourage fine creative writing and artwork and to award excellent efforts in same.

Areas: Fiction, essays, and art.

Description: It is a writing and art contest. Winners are published in an all–student–written issue of *Read* in April.

Eligibility: Sixth – 12th grade males and females.

Important Dates: There is a mid–December deadline for submission.

Competition Origin: 1979.

Guidelines Availability: Contact the sponsor between August and September for guidelines.

Deadline: Entries must be postmarked no later than mid–December.

Winner Notification: Notified in February, published works in April issue of *Read*.

How to Enter: Write to *Read* for guidelines and entry form for the contest.

Judging Criteria: Must be original, unpublished, show true voice, excellent command of English (writing) or materials (art), a spark, and appeal to middle–schoolers.

Judges: Weekly Reader Editorial Staff.

Awards: In each category, first place winners receive $100 and publication; 2nd place winners receive $75; and 3rd place winners receive $50. All receive certificates of excellence, appropriate for framing.

Advice: Entries must be typed, double–spaced, no longer than six pages, and entry coupon must be stapled or taped to back. Art must have return postage and packing materials if student wants it returned.

▲ ^ ▲ ^ ▲ ^ ▲ ^ ▲ ^ ▲ ^ ▲ ^ ▲ ^ ▲ ^ ▲

Competition: The Scholastic Writing Awards.

Sponsor: Alliance for Young Artists and Writers Inc., 555 Broadway, Fourth Floor, New York, NY 10012.

Purpose: To recognize and encourage outstanding writing by students.

Areas: Short story, essay, humor, poetry, dramatic scripts, science fiction/fantasy, and writing portfolios.

Description: This is the National Writing Awards Program, the nation's largest and longest–running writing competition.

Eligibility: Open to all students in grades 7–12.

Important Dates: Write for complete information by November 1.

Competition Origin: 1923.

Guidelines Availability: November 1 from sponsor.

Deadline: Contact sponsor as this varies depending upon geographical region.

Winner Notification: May.

How to Enter: Write for entry materials by November 1. Entries must be accompanied by form.

Judging Criteria: Based upon technical proficiency, style, emergence of writer's voice, and originality.

Judges: Panels of qualified writers, editors, and educators.

Awards: Cash prizes, publication, and scholarships for seniors who submit portfolios.

Advice: Originality is essential to winning.

Competition: The *STORYWORKS* Annual Riddle King Contest.

Sponsor: *STORYWORKS*, Scholastic Inc., 555 Broadway, New York, NY 10012.

Purpose: To build language arts skills and creativity.

Areas: Writing and illustrating.

Description: Participants follow a recipe to write and illustrate a riddle.

Eligibility: Open to all students in grades 6–12.

Important Dates: The contest is announced in the February/March issue of *STORYWORKS* and the deadline for entry is in early April.

Competition Origin: 1993.

Guidelines Availability: See the February/March edition of *STORY-WORKS*.

Deadline: Entries are due in early April.

Winner Notification: Winners are notified by mail in early June.

How to Enter: Follow guidelines as set forth in the February/March issue.

Judging Criteria: Humor, originality, and creativity.

Judges: *STORYWORKS* staff, including the member who writes riddles, known as the Riddle King.

Awards: The grand prize winner will receive a school visit from the Riddle King who will crown that person the Riddle Prince or Princess. There are 101 prizes in all, including autographed books and posters for the finalists and runners–up.

Advice: The riddle recipe changes year–to–year and contestants must use the up–to–date recipe to win. For a copy of the recipe, contact the sponsor in February.

Competition: We are Writers, Too!

Sponsor: Creative With Words Publications, P.O. Box 223226, Carmel, CA 93922.

Purpose: To provide young people an outlet for publication of their original written works.

Areas: Writing and poetry.

Description: Students submit original manuscripts of writing or poetry for possible publication.

Eligibility: Children up to age 19.

Important Dates: June 15 is deadline for submission.

Competition Origin: 1987.

Guidelines Availability: Contact sponsor.

Deadline: June 15 is deadline for submission.

Winner Notification: Approximately two months after deadline, those whose manuscripts have been accepted for publication will be notified with a special congratulatory note.

How to Enter: Submit manuscript with accompanying letter by a responsible adult verifying your age and the authenticity of the work.

Judging Criteria: Creativity, research of topic, and original ideas.

Awards: Up to the top 100 writings are published and offered to the writers and poets at a 20 percent reduction in cost.

Journalism

▼ ▼ ▼ ▼ ▼ ▼ ▼ ▼ ▼ ▼ ▼ ▼ ▼

Competition: Annual *NewsCurrents* Student Editorial Cartoon Contest.

Sponsor: The Annual *NewsCurrents* Student Editorial Cartoon Contest is sponsored by Knowledge Unlimited Inc., publisher of the weekly *NewsCurrents* Current Events Program, P.O. Box 52, Madison, WI 53701.

Purpose: To showcase the complex thinking and communications skills young people are capable of when challenged with effective curricular materials.

Area: Cartooning.

Description: Students submit editorial cartoons. Students may submit as many entries as they wish. There is no entry fee. There are three grade–level categories of competition: K–6, 7–9, and 10–12.

Eligibility: All elementary, middle, and high school students are eligible for the competition.

Important Dates: Entries must be postmarked by March 15.

Guidelines Availability: Entrants must submit original cartoons on any subject of national or international interest. Each entry must include the following information written on the back of the cartoon: student's name, grade, school, school address, school phone number, and the signature of a teacher verifying that the cartoon is the original work of the student.

Deadline: Cartoons may be entered in the contest at any time during the year until March 15.

Winner Notification: Winners will be notified by April 15.

How to Enter: Entries sent after that date will automatically be entered in the next year's contest.

Judging Criteria: Entries will be judged primarily on the basis of originality, clarity of idea, and knowledge of subject. Artistic quality will be considered secondarily.

Judges: Winners will be selected by the editorial staff of *NewsCurrents*.

Awards: One first prize winner, two second prize winners, and at least three third prize winners will be selected from each of the three grade levels of com-

▲ ▲ ▲ ▲ ▲ ▲ ▲ ▲ ▲ ▲ ▲ ▲ ▲

petition. First prize winners will be awarded a $100 U.S. savings bond. Second prize winners will be given a $75 bond, and the third prize winners will receive a $50 bond. First and second prize winners will be published in an issue of the weekly *NewsCurrents* Current Events program, viewed by more than 1 million students. One hundred of the best entries will also be selected to be published in a book by Knowledge Unlimited titled, "Editorial Cartoons By Kids." Students whose cartoons are selected for the book will receive a free copy.

Advice: Judges recommend that cartoons be drawn with black ink on white paper. Use bold lines and make letters large enough to be read easily. Draw the cartoons in a horizontal format. Don't create a cartoon that is nothing more than a simple slogan or a poster. Be thought–provoking and original.

Learn from your mistakes. —12-year-old girl

Competition: National Federation of Press Women High School Journalism Contest.

Sponsor: National Federation of Press Women Youth Projects, Box 99, Blue Springs, MO 64013–0099.

Purpose: To recognize excellent journalistic work in editorials, feature stories, news stories, sports stories, personal columns, feature photos, cartooning, and graphics.

Area: Journalism.

Description: Students compete at national level for cash awards based upon excellence in journalism.

Eligibility: Female students in grades 9–12 who have received a first place award in a state contest.

Important Dates: April 1 is deadline for submission.

Guidelines Availability: Contact sponsor.

Deadline: April 1.

Winner Notification: Annual awards luncheon in June

How to Enter: Contact state affiliate.

Judging Criteria:
Editorial: Local interest for readers, clearness of style, sound reasoning, and effort to influence readers' opinion in what the writer believes is the right direction. An editorial is not a bylined personal opinion column.

Feature: Interest to readers and unusual aspects of the materials or its handling, writing style, and richness of detail and use of quotes, readability, and thoroughness. (Includes personality profiles, human interest, general features, and opinion pieces.)

News: Planning and general organization of story, initiative in obtaining story, quality of newswriting, readability, and impact. An article which presents new information or a new angle.

Sports: Imagination and good application of sportswriting style in advance, follow–up, summary or feature coverage of events; avoiding play–by–play rehash.

Personal column: (Submit 3 columns, two consecutive and one other of student's choice.) Analytical scrutiny, satire, or personal comment/opinion on general or special subjects that entertains and/or educates. May take in–depth knowledge, research, study, or expertise.

Feature photo: Quality of the original print with emphasis on the activity or "story–telling" qualities (not posed shots). Entries are to be candid, human interest pictures of people in their environment (color or black/white).

Cartooning: The entry may be generated by computer graphics or freehand and may be a comic strip, illustration, or political cartoon. The judge will consider the text or caption and the use of concept and artistic style. The subject matter is unrestricted. For example, any political, economic, or social issue may be covered or any human relations issue or any topic. Unsigned work requires an adviser's verification.

Graphics: Single page layout. The entry may be from a desktop publishing project or from the traditional printing production methods. Judges will consider any number of graphic elements, typography, photos, illustrations, and colors. Judging will be on the most creative and effective use of these elements in drawing reader interest and supporting article(s) content. Unsigned work requires an adviser's verification.

Judges: National Federation of Press Women officials.

Awards: $250 for first place; $200 for second place; and $50 for third place in each category.

Competition: Quill and Scroll International Writing and Photo Contest.

Sponsor: Quill and Scroll Society, School of Journalism and Mass Communication, The University of Iowa, Iowa City, IA 52242–1528.

Purpose: To recognize excellence in student journalism.

Areas: Editorial, editorial cartoon, news story, photography/news–feature, photography/sports, feature story, in–depth/individual, in–depth/team, advertisement, and sports story.

Description: Students submit original work which has been published in a high school or professional newspaper.

Eligibility: Currently enrolled high school students.

Important Dates: Entry deadline is in early February.

Guidelines Availability: Contact sponsor.

Deadline: February.

Winner Notification: A complete list of the National Winners appears in the April/May issue of *Quill and Scroll*.

How to Enter: Submit entry with official form and fee of $2.

Judging Criteria: Varies with division.

Judges: Selected by Quill and Scroll Society.

Awards: Winners of the National Newspaper Association Quill and Scroll International Writing and Photo Contest receive a National Award Gold Key Charm. All sweepstakes winners will receive an XL 1900 typewriter courtesy of Smith Corona. The best entry in each category is designated a sweepstakes winner.

Advice: Contact sponsor for official entry form.

Competition: Quill and Scroll National Junior High Writing and Photo Contest.

Sponsor: Quill and Scroll Society, School of Journalism and Mass Communication, The University of Iowa, Iowa City, IA 52242–1528.

Purpose: To recognize excellence in student journalism.

Areas: Editorial, cartoons, news story, feature story, general column, sport story, photography/feature, and photography/sports.

Description: Students submit original work which has been published in a junior high school or professional newspaper.

Eligibility: Currently enrolled junior high school students.

Important Dates: Entry deadline is early February.

Guidelines Availability: Contact sponsor for guidelines.

Deadline: Early February is the deadline for entry.

Winner Notification: A complete list of all winners appears in the April/May issue of *Quill and Scroll* Magazine.

How to Enter: Submit entry with official form and $2 fee.

Judging Criteria: Varies with division.

Judges: Selected by Quill and Scroll Society.

Awards: Winners of the National Junior High Writing and Photo Contest receive a National Award Gold Key Charm. The best entry in each category is designated a sweepstakes winner. All sweepstakes winners will receive a special certificate mounted on a walnut plaque indicating the sweepstakes award for the specific category in which the student earned the special recognition.

Competition: Spider's Corner.

Sponsor: The Cricket Magazine Group, 315 Fifth St., P.O. Box 300, Peru, IL 61354.

Purpose: To encourage literary and artistic creativity and to provide a forum for personal expression.

Areas: Stories, poetry, or art.

Description: The theme of each contest is usually drawn from a poem or story in the current issue.

Eligibility: Readers of any age and of both genders may enter.

Important Dates: Contest entries should be submitted by the 25th of each month.

Competition Origin: The competition began with the launch of *Spider*, a literary magazine for kids 6 to 9 years old in 1994.

Guidelines Availability: The guidelines are stated on page 32 of each issue.

Deadline: Contests are held monthly, entries must be received by the 25th of each month.

Winner Notification: Winners are notified 3 to 4 weeks after the deadline.

How to Enter: Entries must include the reader's name, age, and address, and should be mailed to the sponsor.

Judging Criteria: Stories, poems, and art are judged for their technique, originality, and adherence to contest themes and guidelines.

Judges: The judges are members of *Spider*'s editorial and art departments.

Awards: Winning stories are published in *Spider* magazine.

Mythology and Classical Literature

Competition: Elementary Teachers of Classics National Exam.

Sponsor: Elementary Teachers of Classics, American Classical League, Miami University, Oxford, OH 45056.

Purpose: To acquaint students with mythology and classical literature, including African and Native American myths.

Areas: Mythology and classical literature.

Description: Multiple-choice; machine–scored testing format.

Eligibility: Students in grades 3–9.

Important Dates: Registration is by January 15. Administration of exam is usually in late February or early March.

Guidelines Availability: Contact sponsor.

Deadline: January 15.

Winner Notification: April 30.

How to Enter: Contact sponsor in writing.

Judging Criteria: Performance on exam.

Judges: Sponsor machine scores exams.

Awards: Top 10 percent receive certificates of excellence. Top 5 percent receive bronze medallions.

Playwriting

Competition: Baker's Plays High School Playwriting Contest.

Sponsor: Baker's Plays, 100 Chauncy St., Boston, MA 02111.

Purpose: To encourage creative writing in high school students through the creation of original plays for publication.

Area: Playwriting.

Description: Students submit bound, typed manuscripts with self–addressed, stamped envelopes. Plays are judged on their originality and quality of writing appropriate for a high school audience.

Eligibility: High school students.

Important Dates: Submit plays at the end of January.

Competition Origin: 1990.

Guidelines Availability: Available in September from the sponsor.

Deadline: End of January.

Winner Notification: May.

How to Enter: Write for guidelines.

Judging Criteria: Awards are based on merit, and if no submission warrants an award, no prizes are given.

Awards: First place winner receives $500 and Baker's Plays publishes play. $250 and an Honorable Mention for second place. $100 and an Honorable Mention for third place.

Advice: Content of the plays should include the "high school experience," but may also be about any subject. Plays may be any length but should be written so that they can be reasonably produced on the high school stage.

Competition: Young Playwrights Festival.

Sponsor: Young Playwrights Inc., 321 W. 44th St., Suite 906, New York, NY 10036.

Purpose: To introduce young people to the theater and to encourage self–expression through the art of playwriting.

Area: Playwriting.

Eligibility: The competition is open to playwrights ages 18 and younger.

Competition Origin: Young Playwrights was founded in 1981 by Stephen Sondheim and members of the Dramatists Guild.

Guidelines Availability: Competition guidelines are available year round. This is an annual contest.

Deadline: October 15.

Winner Notification: Notification of preliminary selections will be made in the spring. Final selections will take place early summer.

How to Enter: Obtain guidelines. Submit original playscript according to guidelines. Screenplays and musicals are not eligible. More than one play may be submitted.

Judging Criteria: Selections are based on the quality of writing in play-writing competition. Each playwright receives a written evaluation of the work submitted.

Awards: Production of the play in the Young Playwrights Festival in New York City. Authors will participate in casting and rehearsal of their plays. Playwrights will also receive transportation, housing, royalties, and compli-mentary one–year membership in the Dramatists Guild.

Poetry

We know what we are, but know not what we may be.

—William Shakespeare

Competition: Ann Arlys Bowler Poetry Contest.

Sponsor: Weekly Reader Corp., 245 Long Hill Road, Middletown, CT 06457.

Purpose: To award fine poetic creativity and to encourage writing for middle schoolers and high schoolers.

Area: Poetry — any genre.

Description: This is an annual poetry contest. The winners are published in an all–student written issue of *Read* in April.

Eligibility: 4th through 12th grade.

Competition Origin: The competition was begun in 1989.

Guidelines Availability: Guidelines may be obtained August through September.

Deadline: Mid–December.

Winner Notification: Winners are contacted in February.

How to Enter: Write to "Read Contests" at *Read* Magazine for full guidelines and entry coupon.

Judging Criteria: Entries must be original; not published before; show excellent command of English; have spark; and appeal to middle school readers.

Judges: Weekly Reader Editorial Staff Members.

Awards: Six first place winners receive $100, a silver medal of honor, letter of congratulations from Poet Laureate, and a certificate of excellence. Six semi–finalists receive $50 and a certificate of excellence.

Advice: Entries should be typed, doubled–space, not longer than one page, and the entry coupon must be filled out and stapled to the back.

Competition: Mississippi Valley Poetry Contest.

Sponsor: North American Literary Escadrille, P.O. Box 3188, Rock Island, IL 61204–3188.

Purpose: To promote poetry writing in people of all ages.

Area: Poetry.

Description: Poetry pamphlet is sought by prospective entrants by writing. There are elementary, middle, and high school competition divisions.

Eligibility: Elementary to elderly.

Important Dates: Entry closes April 1 (postmark is final decision).

Competition Origin: 1972.

Guidelines Availability: Year–round availability.

Deadline: April 1 is deadline for entry.

Winner Notification: Within two weeks of Awards Night, or late in April.

How to Enter: Write to sponsor.

Judging Criteria: Quality and intention to fit particular category of entry.

Judges: Judges are selected on their past experiences and credentials.

Awards: $1,400 is given in award monies, with prizes ranging from $50 to $175.

Advice: Individual consideration is given to the poetry sent. It cannot be a poem or poems that have already won.

▼ ▼ ▼ ▼ ▼ ▼ ▼ ▼ ▼ ▼ ▼ ▼ ▼

Competition: National Federation of State Poetry Societies Contest.

Sponsor: National Federation of State Poetry Societies, 3520 State Route 56, Mechanicsburg, OH 43044.

Purpose: To encourage and support the writing of poetry.

Area: Poetry.

Description: One contest for poems of any form, any subject, and up to 32 lines.

Eligibility: Grades 9–12.

Important Dates: Opens January 1 and closes March 15, annually.

Competition Origin: 1959.

Guidelines Availability: December, annually — must send a self-addressed, stamped envelope.

Deadline: Closes March 15, annually.

Winner Notification: Third week of June at the convention .

How to Enter: Send a poem (limit 1 per student) to the National Federation of State Poetry Societies Contests.

Judging Criteria: Judged anonymously by a poet who is a member of NFSPS with expertise in judging.

Judges: They are chosen from prizewinners in the annual contests or their state contests.

Awards: Monetary awards ranging from $40 to $50 are given and selected poems are published.

Advice: Use correct grammar, fresh images, an interesting title, and some real content in your poem.

▲ ▲ ▲ ▲ ▲ ▲ ▲ ▲ ▲ ▲ ▲ ▲ ▲

Competition: Olympic Size Morgan Horse Dreams.

Sponsor: The American Morgan Horse Association, P.O. Box 960, Shelburne, VT 05482–0960.

Purpose: To provide students an opportunity to describe in their own words their "Olympic Size Morgan Horse Dreams." Students are asked to write about what this statement means to them.

Areas: Essays and poetry.

Description: Students write an essay of 1,000 words or less or a poem on the topic "Olympic Size Morgan Horse Dreams."

Eligibility: Participants must not have reached their 22nd birthday as of December 1.

Important Dates: December 1 postmark for essays or poems submitted.

Guidelines Availability: Contact sponsor in early fall.

Deadline: December 1 postmark for essays or poems submitted.

Winner Notification: Upon completion of judging.

How to Enter: The entry form must be attached to your work in order to be considered in the contest.

Judging Criteria: Essays and poetry will be judged on general style, originality, grammar, spelling, and punctuation. The judge's decision will be final.

Judges: American Morgan Horse Association officials.

Awards: Cash awards of $25 will be presented to the winner in both categories: Essay and Poetry. Ribbons will be awarded to the first through fifth place winners in each category.

Advice: Entries will not be returned. Work submitted may be used for promotional purposes by AMHA. Students may see poems or essays in *The Morgan Horse* magazine or on the youth pages in the *AMHA News* and *Morgan Sales Network*.

Competition: Paul A. Witty Outstanding Literature Award.

Sponsor: International Reading Association, Texas Christian University, P.O. Box 32925, Fort Worth, TX 76129.

Purpose: To recognize excellence in prose or poetry.

Areas: Original prose or poetry.

Description: This award of not less than $25 and a certificate of merit will be given to those elementary and secondary students in recognition of qualitative excellence in original prose or poetry of individual writing.

Eligibility: Open to all elementary and secondary students.

Important Dates: Submit by early February.

Competition Origin: Originated in memory of Dr. Paul A. Witty, an author and educator.

Guidelines Availability: Contact sponsor.

Deadline: Early February is deadline for submission.

Winner Notification: By March 15.

How to Enter: Submit poetry or prose with an application to sponsor.

Judging Criteria: Creativity, originality, and beauty of expression.

Judges: International Reading Association committee members.

Awards: Certificate of merit and monetary award of at least $25.

Advice: All works should be original.

Competition: Promising Young Writers Program.

Sponsor: National Council of Teachers of English, 1111 W. Kenyon Road, Urbana, IL 61801–1096.

Purpose: To develop skills in writing.

Areas: Poetry, prose, and essays.

Description: Each participant must submit a "Best Writing Sample" which may be poetry or prose. He or she must also write on an "Impromptu Theme," developed by the Promising Young Writers Advisory Committee. This theme is a common topic on which all students entering the program must write.

Eligibility: Only students who are eighth graders in the current academic school year are eligible to be nominated for the Promising Young Writers Program. The number of nominees allowed from each school is determined by the eighth–grade average daily enrollment.

Competition Origin: 1984.

Guidelines Availability: From the sponsor in the early fall.

Deadline: January 20.

Winner Notification: All certificates will be mailed to school principals, who will be asked to present them to each student who submitted writing samples. Nominating teachers will also be notified.

How to Enter: Complete a nomination form for each student nominee.

Judging Criteria: Papers will be judged on content, purpose, audience, tone, word choice, organization, development, and style. Judges take into account that the writers are eighth–grade students, not professional writers, and that the impromptu papers are written under time constraints.

Judges: Teams of teachers at the state level will judge the writing and select Promising Young Writers.

Awards: Each student who enters and writes will receive a citation. Certificates of Recognition will be awarded to students cited as winners. Certificates of Participation will be awarded to other nominees who write.

Reading and Writing Books

▼ ▽ ▼ ▽ ▼ ▽ ▼ ▽ ▼ ▽ ▼ ▽ ▼ ▽ ▼ ▽

Competition: BOOK IT! National Reading Incentive Program.

Sponsor: Pizza Hut, BOOK IT!, P.O. Box 2999, Wichita, KS 67201.

Purpose: To develop a lifelong love of reading in children.

Area: Reading.

Description: Students in participating classes meet reading goals as established by the classroom teacher to win prizes.

Eligibility: Open to all elementary school classrooms, kindergarten through grade 6.

Important Dates: The program usually begins in early October and runs through the end of February.

Guidelines Availability: Teachers can request guidelines from the sponsor year–round.

Deadline: Teachers must register classes by mid–June.

Winner Notification: Everyone wins. Each classroom teacher may handle awards differently.

How to Enter: Talk to your classroom teacher or principal.

Judging Criteria: Teachers set monthly reading goals which may vary from month to month. Goals may include the numbers of books read, number of pages or chapters read, number of minutes spent reading, etc.

Judges: Classroom teacher sets goals.

Awards: When a child reaches the monthly reading goal, he or she receives a Pizza Hut Award Certificate for a free one–topping Personal Pan Pizza. The child then receives from the restaurant manager a BOOK IT! button and sticker. If the child meets the reading goals for all five months of the program, he or she receives a record of achievement called the Reader's Honor Roll, and an All–Star Reader Medallion with neck ribbon. If all the children in a class meet the reading goals for four of the five months, the entire class receives a pizza party.

Advice: Be sure to discuss this early with your teacher or school principal.

△ ▲ △ ▲ △ ▲ △ ▲ △ ▲ △ ▲ △ ▲ △ ▲

Competition: Kids Are Authors.

Sponsor: Trumpet Book Fairs, 801 94th Ave. North, St. Petersburg, FL 33702.

Purpose: To encourage students to interact and cooperate as a team, while at the same time developing reading, writing, and language skills.

Area: Picture books written and illustrated for children.

Description: Kids Are Authors is a picture book writing and illustration competition. Each entry must be the result of a cooperative effort of three or more students. The winning entry is published in a hardcover edition by Willowisp Press.

Eligibility: Groups of three or more students in grades K–8.

Important Dates: Deadline for entries is March 1.

Competition Origin: 1986.

Guidelines Availability: Rules and entry forms available throughout the year.

Deadline: Entries must be postmarked by March 1 to enter the current year's competition. All entries postmarked after March 1 are automatically entered in the following year's competition.

Winner Notification: By May 15.

How to Enter: Groups of three or more students (grades K–8) whose school has held a book fair with Trumpet Book Fairs that school year can enter this competition by writing and illustrating their own, previously unpublished, original picture book. Entries must consist of 8 to 12 original illustrations, with separate accompanying pages of text maximum 50 words per page, typed (computer–generated OK) or handwritten. No more than 24 total pages. Each entry must be accompanied by a completed official entry form. Write to the address above for more information.

Judging Criteria: Entries will be judged on originality, story content, illustrative quality, and compatibility of text and illustrations.

Judges: Judges are selected by Trumpet Book Fairs from professionals in the fields of children's literature, art, and education.

Awards: The winning school receives $1,000 and the teacher or project coordinator gets $250 in books. The winning students receive copies of the published book, an award ceremony, T–shirts, award medallions, and framed certificates. Up to 10 honor awards may be selected; honor winners receive $100 for their schools and framed certificates.

Advice: Start with a group brainstorming session on story ideas. Once the group has come to a consensus on the story line, the children should begin asking themselves what is the best way to express that concept through works and illustrations. Introduce children to various art techniques and allow them to experiment with the one that works best for them. Bold images in bright colors often work best. Project coordinators and students may want to read and review previous Kids Are Authors winners for inspiration.

Competition: The National Written and Illustrated By ... Awards Contest for Students.

Sponsor: Landmark Editions Inc., P.O. Box 4469, Kansas City, MO 64127.

Purpose: To encourage and celebrate the creative efforts of students.

Areas: Writing and illustrating books.

Description: This contest inspires and motivates students to write, illustrate, and assemble original books, giving them the opportunity to utilize their creative skills and talents. Each participant must write and illustrate an original book in any genre, either prose or poetry, with illustrations in any medium, but must remain two–dimensional and flat to the page.

Eligibility: Six to 19 years of age, boys and girls.

Competition Origin: 1985.

Guidelines Availability: Year-round.

Deadline: May 1.

Winner Notification: October 15.

How to Enter: For a free copy of the contest rules and guidelines, send a self–addressed business–sized envelope (#10), stamped with $.64 postage to contest sponsor.

Judging Criteria: Originality, skills in writing and illustrating, and how the text and art combine to make a total publishable book.

Judges: Books are judged by a distinguished national panel of educators, editors of publications, and authors and illustrators of juvenile literature.

Awards: All–expenses–paid trip to Kansas City, MO, where the staff at Landmark assists the winners in the final production phases of their books which will be published and royalties paid annually on the sales of the books.

Advice: Follow the contest format according to the rules and guidelines. Take care that the writing and illustrating both are given careful attention.

Competition: Publish–a–Book Contest.

Sponsor: Raintree/Steck–Vaughn Publishers, P.O. Box 27010, Austin, TX 78755.

Purpose: To allow students an opportunity for exploration of their own creativity in writing and for publication of fiction and non–fiction.

Areas: Fiction and non–fiction writing.

Description: Students write a fiction or non–fiction story and compete for prizes.

Eligibility: Open to all students in grades 2–6.

Important Dates: Entries must be postmarked by January 31.

Guidelines Availability: After September 1 from sponsor.

Deadline: January 31 is deadline for entering.

Winner Notification: Selected by May 1; winners and sponsors notified by phone or mail.

How to Enter: Entries for grades 2–3 should be between 300 and 500 words, and entries for grades 4–6 should be between 700 and 900 words in length. All entries should be typed, double–spaced. The student must put his or her name, home address, and telephone number on the first page only of the entry. A separate top cover sheet must contain the following information: (a) the student's name, home address, and telephone number with area code; (b) the student's current grade level; (c) the sponsor's name; and (d) the name, address, and telephone number (with area code) of the sponsor's school or library.

Judging Criteria: Appeal and originality of work.

Judges: Selected by sponsor.

Awards: Grand Prizes: Raintree/Steck–Vaughn publishes the grand prize entries in January. Each grand prize winner receives a $500 advance against an author royalty contract, as well as 10 copies of the published book. The sponsor of each of the winning entrants will receive 20 free books from the Raintree/Steck–Vaughn catalog. Each honorable mention winner will receive $25, and his or her sponsor will receive 10 free books from the

Raintree/Steck–Vaughn catalog.

Advice: Each entry may have only one author, and each author may submit only one entry. Illustrated manuscripts will not be accepted, as the winning stories will be professionally illustrated.

Short Stories

Competition: Adlyn M. Keffer Memorial Short Story Writing Contest.

Sponsor: Adlyn M. Keffer Memorial Short Story Writing Contest, 984 Roelofs Road, Yardley, PA 19067.

Purpose: To encourage short story writing.

Area: Short story writing.

Description: Three copies of the story must be submitted — typed on white 8½ by 11-inch paper, double–spaced and on one side of the page only. Story must not exceed 2,000 words. Number of words in story should be placed in upper right hand corner of title page. Only one entry will be accepted from each contestant. Story must be original. No identifying marks or names shall appear on manuscript or title page. On a separate page put title of story, name and address of author, and whether the author is an adult or of junior age. On this page also indicate membership in a story league or youth group, including the name of the school and sponsor's name if applicable.

Eligibility: There is a separate youth contest for students in grades 7 through 12 with three prizes of $20, $15, and $10. There may be up to three honorable mentions. All contest rules for the adult contest apply to the youth contest.

Important Dates: Contest begins January 1 and ends at midnight March 31.

Guidelines Availability: Contact the National Story League for guidelines.

Deadline: Deadline for submission is March 31st.

How to Enter: All entries are to be sent to the contest chairman.

Judging Criteria:
1. Originality: entirely author's creation.
2. Tellability: suitable for telling.
3. Title: interesting, suitable, brief.
4. Beginning: makes one want to continue.
5. Plot: simple with only one story.
6. Characters: real, vivid so that one may visualize and hear them.
7. Language: expressive vocabulary.
8. Grammar: correct spelling and sentence structure.
9. Ending: story comes to a climax, definite, pointed, and clear.

Judges: There shall be three judges, one appointed by each district president with the approval of the NSL president. A district judge may request of his or her district president the appointment of an assistant with the youth contest, if needed. Judges' names will be published in *STORY ART* Magazine when winners are announced.

Awards: Three prizes of $25, $15, and $10 may be awarded. There may be up to three honorable mentions.

Advice: All stories submitted become the property of the National Story League. No manuscripts will be returned. Author retains all rights except first publication rights of the stories published in *STORY ART* magazine. All rights revert to author if story is not published in *STORY ART* Magazine or one year from the time stories are received by *STORY ART* Magazine.

Take the time to do it; you might actually win!

—14-year-old boy

Competition: *Seventeen* Magazine Annual Fiction Contest.

Sponsor: *Seventeen,* 850 Third Ave., New York, NY 10022.

Purpose: To encourage young fiction writers.

Area: Fictional short stories.

Description: Students submit original fiction short stories.

Eligibility: Open to all young people between the ages of 13 and 21 as of April 30 of contest year.

Important Dates: April 30 is deadline for submission.

Competition Origin: 1944.

Guidelines Availability: They are published in the November issue or available by sending self–addressed stamped envelope to the sponsor.

Deadline: April 30 is the deadline for entries.

Winner Notification: Late fall.

How to Enter: Send in previously published story of 3,000 words or less; include name and birthdate on the first page, upper right hand corner.

Judging Criteria: Quality of writing and storytelling techniques.

Awards: $1,000 first prize; $500 second prize; $250 third prize; and $50 honorable mentions.

Advice: Manuscripts will not be returned.

Speech and Debate

Competition: Freedoms Foundation National Awards Program.

Sponsor: Freedoms Foundation at Valley Forge, Rt. 23, Valley Forge, PA 19482–0706.

Purpose: To publicly honor and recognize the exceptional efforts of individuals, organizations, corporations, and schools who promote, through words or deeds, an understanding of responsible citizenship and the benefits of a free society.

Areas: Most youth category entries are in the form of written essays and speeches. However, projects for individual achievement or involvement in communities are also welcome.

Description: Eligible material must have been written, developed, or released during the May 1 to May 1 awards year.

Eligibility: Open to all citizens and legal residents of the U.S. grade K–12.

Important Dates: May 1 is deadline for entry. Award ceremonies are conducted by regional volunteer chapters beginning October 15.

Competition Origin: 1949.

Guidelines Availability: Year–round.

Deadline: May 1 of each year.

Winner Notification: Awardees will be announced by September 1 of each year.

How to Enter: Submit typed copy of essay or speech. Activities should be put in a ring binder or scrap book with substantiating materials.

Judging Criteria: A nomination must relate to one or more of the basic American rights set forth in the *American Credo* or the obligations outlined in the *Bill of Responsibilities*, both of which are Freedom Foundation documents available from the sponsor.

Judges: National Awards Jury is comprised of chief and associate State Supreme Court justices, executive offices from National Veteran Service and civic clubs, veterans, or educational organizations.

Awards: Top recipient in Youth Category receives $100 U.S. Saving Bond and framed George Washington Honor Medal. All other recipients receive a George Washington Honor Medal.

Advice: Winning entries from other local/national contests are eligible. Entries may not be the product of classroom assignments.

Competition: National Junior Forensic League.

Sponsor: National Forensic League, Box 38, Ripon, WI 54971.

Purpose: To honor junior high school and middle school students involved in speech.

Areas: Debate and speech.

Description: Students compete locally to accumulate points to qualify for national honors.

Eligibility: Grades 6–9.

Important Dates: None, program runs throughout the school year.

Competition Origin: NJFL began in 1995.

Guidelines Availability: September 1 of each school year.

Deadline: Honors awarded throughout the school year.

How to Enter: Schools may join NJFL. Students speak publicly to qualify for NJFL membership and honors.

Judging Criteria: Determined locally.

Judges: Determined locally.

Awards: Diplomas, seals, pins.

Competition: National High School Oratorical Competition.

Sponsor: The American Legion National Headquarters, P.O. Box 1055, Indianapolis, IN 46206–1055.

Purpose: To develop a deeper knowledge and appreciation of the Constitution of the United States on the part of high school students. Other objectives are those of leadership, the ability to think and speak clearly and intelligently, and the preparation for the acceptance of the duties and responsibilities, the rights and privileges of American citizenship.

Area: Speeches.

Description: Prepared orations must be based upon the Constitution of the United States. Assigned topics which follow the prepared orations are also based on the Constitution. All contestants at any one contest speak on the same assigned topics. Prepared orations must be eight to 10 minutes in length, with the assigned topics running from three to five minutes.

Eligibility: Eligible participants should be citizens of the United States currently enrolled in high school.

Important Dates: Department (state–level) contests are usually held during the month of March. Dates for the National Regionals and Sectionals, and the National Finals Contest are determined by The American Legion National Americanism Commission and are published in the annual Oratorical Contest Rules brochure. These contests are usually held during the month of April.

Competition Origin: 1938.

Guidelines Availability: Write to The American Legion National Headquarters.

Deadline: Set by local and/or State American Legion Headquarters.

Winner Notification: Winners are notified at each level of competition.

How to Enter: Contact your local, state, or National American Legion Headquarters, The Americanism and Children and Youth Division.

Judging Criteria: Oratorical contests are often held before high school student bodies, thus affording students the opportunity of listening to the interpretation of certain articles and sections of the Constitution.

Judges: Each contest uses five judges. Their qualifications are considered carefully. Judges are typically from the legal profession, educators, the media, and the clergy.

Awards: A National Scholarship fund of $138,000, provided by The American Legion Life Insurance Committee, is divided as follows: each Legion Department (state) winner who participates in National Contest at the regional level will receive a $1,000 scholarship. Each Regional winner who participates in the sectional and does not qualify for the finals, will receive an additional $3,000 scholarship. Each contestant in the National Finals will be ranked according to the opinion of the judges and will receive scholarships in the following amounts: first, $18,000; second, $16,000; third, $14,000; and fourth $12,000. Many more thousands of dollars in scholarships are awarded each year by Departments of The American Legion, their districts, and posts.

Advice: The National Organization of The American Legion will pay the travel cost of department winners and their chaperones as they progress in the national competition. All contestants must be accompanied by a chaperone.

Competition: United Nations Pilgrimage for Youth.

Sponsor: The Odd Fellows and Rebekahs, P.O. Box 1778, Palm Harbor, FL 34682–1778.

Purpose: To study and learn about the United Nations.

Area: Global issues.

Description: Students complete a U.N. exam, submit an essay, and/or participate in a speech contest. Selected winners receive an expense–paid trip to New York City.

Eligibility: Open to students ages 16–17.

Important Dates: Dates vary. Make application for more information.

Competition Origin: June 1950.

Guidelines Availability: Contact local Odd Fellow and/or Rebekah Lodges.

Winner Notification: Prior to June trip.

How to Enter: Contact local Odd Fellow and/or Rebekah Lodges.

Judging Criteria: Applications are reviewed by selecting committees for evidence of scholarship, leadership, character, extra–curricular activities, concern for community welfare, interest in world affairs, and general fitness to participate in the program.

Awards: Each year, during June and July, North American students travel by bus to and from New York City, visiting monuments and places of interest on the way. The Odd Fellows and Rebekahs sponsor the entire cost of the tour. They are housed four to a room in New York, sharing with students from as far away as Australia, Denmark, Finland, Germany, Norway, Sweden, and Switzerland. The week–long schedule includes four half day visits to the United Nations where students are allowed to listen to behind–the–scenes briefings on specialized U.N. agencies and departments, witness a council or committee in action, see business conducted in the six official languages of the U.N., and take a guided tour.

Advice: Students who are interested should contact their local Odd Fellow and/or Rebekah Lodges.

Spelling and Vocabulary

Competition: The Scripps Howard National Spelling Bee.

Sponsor: Scripps Howard National Spelling Bee, P.O. Box 5380, Cincinnati, OH 45201.

Purpose: To help students improve their spelling, increase their vocabularies, acquire concepts, learn language development, and improve reading skills that will benefit them all their lives.

Area: Spelling.

Description: The program takes place on two levels: local and national. The only way students may participate in the National Spelling Bee is through an authorized sponsor in their area. The majority of sponsors are either daily, weekly, or Sunday newspapers. Authorized sponsors organize programs in their locales, often in cooperation with educators, businesses, and community organizations. These sponsors send their champions to the national finals. The national program is coordinated by the Scripps Howard National Spelling Bee office, operating year–round out of Scripps Howard's corporate headquarters in Cincinnati, OH.

Eligibility: Students who have not reached their 16th birthday on or before the date of the national finals and who have not passed beyond the eighth grade at the time of their school finals are eligible to compete. Each contestant at the national finals is the champion of his or her sponsor's final spelling bee. In most areas, students qualify for the sponsor's final spelling bee by winning preliminary competitions that include a combination of classroom, grade level, school, school district, and county spelling bees. Dates for these competitions vary by sponsor, but must be completed by, and a national participant chosen by April 10.

Important Dates: The 2–day national competition is held on Wednesday and Thursday of the week in which Memorial Day is celebrated.

Guidelines Availability: Contact local sponsor for details.

Winner Notification: Upon completion of competition.

How to Enter: Contact the the local authorized sponsor where available.

Judging Criteria: The Scripps Howard National Spelling Bee is an oral competition conducted in rounds until only one speller remains. Each speller has been assigned a number and will spell in this order. A speller who correctly spells his or her word stays seated on the stage and waits for the next round. If the speller misspells his or her given word, that speller is eliminated from the competition.

Awards: The first place winner receives a $5,000 cash prize and an engraved loving cup trophy from Scripps Howard Inc., choice of the Anniversary Edition of the *New Encyclopedia Britannica* or the *Great Books of the Western World* from Encyclopedia Britannica, and a $1,000 U.S. Savings Bond from Merriam–Webster. The second place prize is $4,000.

Competition: The WordMasters Challenge.

Sponsor: WordMasters, 213 E. Allendale Ave., Allendale, NJ 07401.

Purpose: To encourage growth in vocabulary and verbal reasoning.

Area: Word comprehension.

Description: Students are challenged to complete analogies based on relationships among the words they have learned through vocabulary development. The contest consists of three 20–minute analogy–solving contests.

Eligibility: Open to all students in grades 3–8.

Important Dates: Meets are scheduled during December, February, and April.

Guidelines Availability: Year–round availability from sponsor.

Deadline: Schools must register teams by mid–October.

Winner Notification: At the conclusion of each academic year.

How to Enter: Schools wishing to participate must register and pay entrance fee to the sponsor by mid–October.

Judging Criteria: Accuracy of answers.

Judges: Participating teachers and WordMasters officials.

Awards: Medal and certificates of merit.

Mathematics

Never turn down a good competition—they
are the best character builders around!
—14-year-old girl

Competition: American Mathematics Competitions (AMC).

Sponsor: The American Mathematics Competitions, 1740 Vine St., University of Nebraska, Lincoln, NE 68588–0658.

Purpose: To provide a friendly challenge to students and also to offer an opportunity to recognize mathematical talent.

Area: Mathematics.

Description: The AJHSME is a 25–question, 40–minute multiple–choice pre–algebra examination open to students in eighth grade and below. There are two examinations open to all junior high and senior high school students — the American Junior High School Mathematics Examination (AJHSME) and the American High School Mathematics Examination (AHSME).

Eligibility: All junior high and senior high school students.

Important Dates: Junior high school test is administered on the Thursday before Thanksgiving. High school is administered on the Thursday before the third Monday in February.

Competition Origin: The AJHSME was first given in 1985. The AHSME was first given in 1950.

Guidelines Availability: Early in the school year.

Deadline: Junior high school deadline for registration is mid–October; high school deadline for registration is mid–January.

Winner Notification: Upon receipt and scoring of exams.

How to Enter: Contact sponsor.

Judging Criteria: Proficiency in pre-algebra and pre-calculus concepts.

Judges: Electronically scored in Lincoln, NE.

Awards: The top participants are recognized as Honor Roll students. The AHSME Honor Roll students are invited to take the American Invitational Mathematics Examination in March, and the top 140 AHSME–AIME students are invited to take the USA Mathematical Olympiad in April.

Competition: American Regions Mathematics League Competitions.

Sponsor: American Regions Mathematics League, R.D. 5, Box 133, Kings Ridge Road, Mahopac, NY 10541.

Purpose: To make students more comfortable with their abilities and introduce them to new and exciting areas of math.

Area: Mathematics.

Description: The annual competition is designed for both teams and individuals on the teams. The team round consists of short–answer questions the team members work on cooperatively. The Power Round forces the team to use various methods of mathematical analysis and proof; members must then expand and generalize from the topic. The conclusions are put together in the form of a report. The Individual Round allows participants to work independently on several questions within a mandated time frame. The Relay Round sets up "subteams" within a team: the answer to one team member's question is used by another to answer the next. Credit is only given if the final team member answers correctly.

Eligibility: Secondary students from all 50 states and from Canada.

Important Dates: Contact sponsor for dates each year.

Competition Origin: 1975.

Guidelines Availability: Contact sponsor in writing.

Deadline: Varies each year.

Winner Notification: Each stage of competition.

How to Enter: Write to the sponsor for entry information.

Judging Criteria: Varies with each competition. Accuracy of answers is key factor.

Judges: American Regions Mathematics League officials and volunteers.

Awards: All participants receive a certificate for participation. Other prizes include trophies and plaques.

Competition: Continental Mathematics League.

Sponsor: Continental Mathematics League, Box 2196, St. James, NY 11780.

Purpose: To enhance students' mathematical problem solving skills.

Area: Mathematics.

Description: There are five meets held throughout the year, featuring six questions per meet.

Eligibility: Open to all students in grades 2–12.

Important Dates: Register by early October.

Competition Origin: 1980.

Guidelines Availability: Contact sponsor in March.

Winner Notification: March.

How to Enter: Register by contacting the sponsor.

Awards: Medals and certificates are awarded to the winners.

Competition: MATHCOUNTS.

Sponsor: MATHCOUNTS Foundation, 1420 King St., Alexandria, VA 22314.

Purpose: To promote seventh and eighth grade math achievement through grass–roots involvement in every U.S. state and territory.

Areas: Estimation/approximation, computation, equivalent expressions, statistics, probability, measurement, geometry, number theory, scientific notation, equations/inequalities, consumer math, and algebra topics.

Description: MATHCOUNTS is a national math coaching and competition program that promotes seventh and eighth grade math achievement through grass–roots involvement in every U.S. state and territory.

Eligibility: Students at the seventh and eighth grade levels.

Competition Origin: MATHCOUNTS was founded in 1983 by the National Society of Professional Engineers and the CNA Insurance Companies, the General Motors Foundation, the Intel Foundation, Texas Instruments Inc., the National Council of Teachers of Mathematics, and the National Aeronautics and Space Administration.

Guidelines Availability: From sponsor in the early fall.

Deadline: Early November.

Winner Notification: At each level of competition.

How to Enter: School completes and forwards application.

Judging Criteria: Vary with math–related area of competition.

Judges: Professionals in mathematics and related areas.

Awards: At all levels of the competition appropriate recognition and/or awards are given to winning individuals, teams, coaches, and schools. The top four individuals in each state–level competition receives an all–expenses–paid trip to Washington, DC, to compete in the national competition. At the national competition, the first, second, and third place individuals will receive $8,000, $6,000, and $4,000 college scholarships, respectively. The student scoring the highest in the written portion of the competition is awarded a $2,000 college scholarship. Each member of the winning team receives a $2,000 college scholarship.

Competition: Mathematical Olympiads for Elementary and Middle Schools.

Sponsor: Mathematical Olympiads for Elementary and Middle Schools, 125 Merle Ave., Oceanside, NY 11572.

Purpose: To provide opportunities for teachers and children to engage in creative problem solving activities throughout the school year.

Areas: Mathematics, enrichment areas, and special topics.

Description: Five contests (Olympiads) are administered during the school year, beginning in November and, thereafter, at monthly intervals.

Eligibility: Students need to be in sixth grade or lower. Most students are in grades 4–6. Some very capable children in grades 1–3 participate.

Important Dates: Registration deadline: September 30. First contest is given in November.

Competition Origin: Competition began during the 1978–1979 school year.

Guidelines Availability: Guidelines may be obtained in June.

Deadline: September 30.

Winner Notification: Awards are announced in April for both team and individual awards. Olympiads do not have first place, second place, etc. Instead, categories such as outstanding achievement and high achiever are recognized.

How to Enter: Write for registration form and other information.

Judging Criteria: Each Olympiad contains five open–ended questions with a time limit on each. If a student gets a correct answer, he or she receives a point and his or her team is credited with one point.

Judges: An Appeals Committee reviews student appeals.

Awards: Certificate to each participant, cloth Olympiad Patches to top 50 percent of all participants, "silver" or "gold" pins to top 10 percent, Medallions to children with perfect score (25 points); team plaques to 10 percent of all teams, high achievement certificates to teams in the next 10 percent, meritorious certificates to fifth grade and fourth grade teams.

Competition: National Mathematics League Contests.

Sponsor: National Mathematics League, P.O. Box 9459, Coral Springs, FL 33075.

Purpose: To encourage students to participate actively in mathematics and to continue their mathematical studies.

Areas: Calculus, pre–calculus, algebra II, geometry, algebra I, pre–algebra, and sixth grade mathematics.

Description: School teams compete in a series of five mathematics contests.

Eligibility: Student must be currently enrolled in a course corresponding to area of competition.

Important Dates: Contests are held in the spring of each year.

Guidelines Availability: Contact sponsor in early fall for guidelines.

Deadline: October 31.

Winner Notification: Announced and mailed in the final newsletter, published in late spring.

How to Enter: Determine a team sponsor and submit application form with fees.

Judging Criteria: Objective questions scored by team sponsor.

Judges: Team sponsors score using test author's answer key.

Awards: Each school receives a ribbon for its first and second place student in each division. The schools with the highest cumulative scores in each division receive an engraved plaque, and top scoring individuals receive rosette ribbons. A special sweepstakes plaque is awarded to the top 10 high schools. Winners are determined by totaling the school team scores in algebra I, geometry, algebra II, and pre–calculus.

Advice: Scientific calculators may be used only the fifth contest in each series.

▼ ▽ ▼ ▽ ▼ ▽ ▼ ▽ ▼ ▽ ▼ ▽ ▼ ▽

Competition: Scholastic *DynaMath* Scavenger Hunt.

Sponsor: Scholastic *DynaMath* Magazine, Scholastic Inc., 555 Broadway, New York, NY 10012–3999.

Purpose: To find math–related information about TV commercials.

Area: Mathematics.

Description: Subscribers are asked to find math–related answers to five questions about TV commercials.

Eligibility: Open to all *DynaMath* readers. Each class should work together as a group and submit one entry for judging.

Important Dates: Contest deadline is November 15.

Competition Origin: 1984.

Guidelines Availability: See fall issues of *DynaMath*.

Deadline: November 15.

Winner Notification: Announced in a spring issue of *DynaMath*.

How to Enter: Entry details are available in the October issue of *DynaMath*.

Judging Criteria: Based upon the following: number of correct answers, neatness, creativity, and level of research.

Judges: *DynaMath* staff.

Awards: First prize winners receive calculators and t–shirts for the entire class (including teacher). Runners–up receive Scholastic gift certificates for teachers and classroom.

▲ ▲ ▲ ▲ ▲ ▲ ▲ ▲ ▲ ▲ ▲ ▲ ▲ ▲

Competition: TEAMS (Tests of Engineering Aptitude, Mathematics, and Science).

Sponsor: Junior Engineering Technical Society Inc. (JETS), 1420 King St., Suite 405, Alexandria, VA 22314–2794.

Purpose: To enable teams of high school students to learn team development and problem–solving skills.

Areas: Mathematics and science.

Description: Teams participate in an open–book, open–discussion environment to solve real–world engineering problems. Teams learn how the mathematics and science concepts they are learning in high school are applied to real–world problems. TEAMS problems focus on all areas of mathematics and science, as well as on computer fundamentals, graphics interpretation, and English/communication skills and concepts.

Eligibility: All students in grades 9 through 12 may participate. Teams are made up of between four and eight team members. Varsity and Junior Varsity divisions are available at most sites.

Important Dates: TEAMS is a one–day, two–part event held between early February and mid–March each year. Schools may begin registering teams beginning in September.

Competition Origin: TEAMS was established in 1979.

Guidelines Availability: Information is updated each summer for the following year's TEAMS program. Information is available year–round.

Deadline: The deadline for registering for TEAMS varies by site, but generally is about one month before the competition date. All registered schools receive coaching and practice materials, so the earlier schools register, the more time they will have to prepare.

Winner Notification: Teams usually receive local (regional) results on competition day. State rankings are announced one week after the last competition date. National rankings are announced by mid–April.

How to Enter: Schools that have not participated before should contact JETS for information on the competition site nearest them. All schools register directly with the competition host.

Judging Criteria: TEAMS consists of a two–part exam. Part 1 is multiple–choice and is scored on competition day. Part 1 determines both regional and state rankings. Top–scoring teams in each of nine Varsity and nine Junior Varsity divisions in each state are eligible for national ranking, which is based on part 2, the subjective portion of the exam. Part 2 is scored by a panel of engineers determined by JETS and the TEAMS problem development coordinator.

Awards: Awards are given for regional, state, and national recognition. Regional and state awards vary by site and state; national awards are given by JETS and vary from year to year.

Advice: Register early in order to receive coaching and preparation materials in time to make them useful.

Competition: U.S.A. Mathematical Talent Search (USAMTS).

Sponsor: U.S.A. Mathematical Talent Search, Department of Mathematics, Box 130, Rose-Hulman Institute of Technology, 5500 Wabash Ave., Terre Haute, IN 47803.

Purpose: To encourage and assist the development of problem solving skills of talented high school students.

Area: Mathematics.

Description: The USAMTS consists of four rounds with each round featuring five problems. Through the regular USAMTS column in *Consortium* and through direct invitations, the participating high school students are asked to submit solutions to at least two of the problems of each round. The problems are published and distributed so as to allow at least four weeks for the preparation of the solutions by participants.

Eligibility: Open to all high school students.

Competition Origin: This competition was initiated in 1989.

Guidelines Availability: Available from the sponsor.

Deadline: The deadlines for each round are at least one month from the date of publication.

Winner Notification: At the end of each round, in addition to the solutions and a copy of the completed individual USAMTS cover sheet, each participant receives a copy of a newsletter, which provides an update on the competition, as well as other valuable information.

How to Enter: Contact the sponsor for details.

Judging Criteria: Accuracy of solutions.

Judges: USAMTS officials.

Awards: Students who present an exceptionally nice solution to a particular problem receive recognition among the Commended Solvers of that problem. These students are listed in the newsletter along with criteria for their selection. In addition, those who are commended solvers for all five problems of a round are recognized as the Problemist of the Round and receive special prizes.

Science

Success seems to be connected with action.
Successful people keep moving. They make
mistakes, but they don't quit.
—Conrad Hilton

Chemistry

▼ ▼ ▼ ▼ ▼ ▼ ▼ ▼ ▼ ▼ ▼ ▼ ▼ ▼ ▼ ▼

Competition: U.S. National Chemistry Olympiad.

Sponsor: American Chemical Society, 1155 16th St. N.W., Washington, DC 20036.

Purpose: To promote excellence in chemistry, as well as select four students to represent the United States at the International Chemistry Olympiad (IChO).

Area: Chemistry.

Description: The U.S. National Chemistry Olympiad (USNCO) is a multi–tiered competition for high school students. The local section competitions are usually held from late February to early April and consist of a locally determined competition such as a written exam, a laboratory practical, or a science fair. The best students from the local competition participate in the three–part, four–and–one–half–hour national exam in late April. The national exam consists of a 60–question multiple-choice section, an eight–question free–response section, and a two–exercise laboratory practical.

Eligibility: Open to all high school chemistry students.

Important Dates: Local competitions are held February–April; the national exam is given in late April.

Guidelines Availability: Contact local American Chemical Society.

Deadline: Varies at each level of competition.

How to Enter: Students who are interested in this competition should check with their chemistry teacher to see if their school already participates. ACS local sections generally contact chemistry teachers about participating in this program. If information on participation in your area is unavailable through your teacher or school's science department, please call the ACS Olympiad program.

Judging Criteria: Objective examination.

Awards: Of the approximately 1,000 students taking this exam, 20 are invited to attend a two–week study camp, held at the U.S. Air Force Academy in mid–June. At the study camp, the students undergo an intense schedule of lectures, laboratory exercises, and exams. The top four students are selected from the camp to compete in the International Chemistry Olympiad in mid–July.

▲ ▲ ▲ ▲ ▲ ▲ ▲ ▲ ▲ ▲ ▲ ▲ ▲ ▲ ▲ ▲

Engineering

Competition: National Engineering Design Challenge (NEDC).

Sponsor: Junior Engineering Technical Society Inc. (JETS), 1420 King Street, Suite 405, Alexandria, VA 22314–2794.

Purpose: To apply the math, science, and technology concepts students learn in classrooms to a real engineering problem.

Areas: Science, math, and technology.

Description: Originally funded by the National Science Foundation, the National Engineering Design Challenge challenges teams of high school students, often working with an engineering adviser, to design, fabricate, and demonstrate a working solution to a societal need.

Eligibility: All students in grades 9 through 12 may participate. Teams may consist of as many students as a school wishes. In competition, however, only five students may present.

Important Dates: The NEDC problem materials are available to schools beginning in mid–August. Regional and state competitions are generally held in January and February. The national competition in Washington, DC, is held in late March or early April.

Competition Origin: NEDC was established through a grant from the National Science Foundation in 1989. It was founded by JETS, the National Society of Professional Engineers, and the National Talent Network of the Educational Information and Resource Center.

Guidelines Availability: Program materials are available beginning in mid–August. Schools must register at least six weeks before their scheduled competition date, in order to have enough time to prepare for competition. NEDC materials are available year–round for schools that wish to use them as curricular materials.

Deadline: The deadline for registering for NEDC varies by site, but generally is about six weeks before the competition date. Schools may purchase the program materials beginning in mid–August (directly through JETS) and may register for competition later.

Winner Notification: Regional, state, and national competition results are announced on the respective competition days.

How to Enter: Schools that have not participated before should contact JETS and register for competition with the NEDC coordinator nearest them.

Judging Criteria: Judging panels at NEDC events generally consist of three to five engineers and educators. Judges are selected by the NEDC coordinators.

Awards: Awards are given for regional, state, and national recognition. Regional and state awards vary by site and state; national awards vary as well, but have consisted of trophies, medallions, t–shirts and cash awards.

Advice: Purchase the materials package as early as possible. Registering for competition can be done at a later date. Contact JETS for more information about the NEDC.

I always had something to shoot for each year—to jump one inch farther.

—Jackie Joyner–Kersee

Competition: TEAMS (Tests of Engineering Aptitude, Mathematics, and Science).

Sponsor: Junior Engineering Technical Society Inc. (JETS), 1420 King St., Suite 405, Alexandria, VA 22314–2794.

Purpose: To enable teams of high school students to learn team development and problem–solving skills.

Areas: Mathematics and science.

Description: Teams participate in an open–book, open–discussion environment to solve real–world engineering problems. Teams learn how the mathematics and science concepts they are learning in high school are applied to real–world problems. TEAMS problems focus on all areas of mathematics and science, as well as on computer fundamentals, graphics interpretation, and English/communication skills and concepts.

Eligibility: All students in grades 9 through 12 may participate. Teams are made up of between four and eight team members. Varsity and Junior Varsity divisions are available at most sites.

Important Dates: TEAMS is a one–day, two–part event held between early February and mid–March each year. Schools may begin registering teams beginning in September.

Competition Origin: TEAMS was established in 1979.

Guidelines Availability: Information is updated each summer for the following year's TEAMS program. Schools or students may request information year–round.

Deadline: The deadline for registering for TEAMS varies by site, but generally is about one month before the competition date. All registered schools receive coaching and practice materials, so the earlier schools register, the more time they will have to prepare.

Winner Notification: Teams usually receive local (regional) results on competition day. State rankings are announced one week after the last competition date. National rankings are announced by mid–April.

How to Enter: Schools that have not participated before should contact JETS for information on the competition site nearest them. All schools register directly with the competition host.

Judging Criteria: TEAMS consists of a two–part exam. Part 1 is multiple–choice and is scored on competition day. Part 1 determines both regional and state rankings. Top–scoring teams in each of nine Varsity and nine Junior Varsity divisions in each state are eligible for national ranking, which is based on part 2, the subjective portion of the exam. Part 2 is scored by a panel of engineers determined by JETS and the TEAMS problem development coordinator.

Awards: Awards are given for regional, state, and national recognition. Regional and state awards vary by site and state; national awards are given by JETS and vary from year to year.

Advice: Register early, in order to receive coaching and preparation materials in time to make them useful.

Competition: The Thomas Edison/Max McGraw Scholarship Program.

Sponsor: Edison/McGraw Scholarship Program, National Science Education Leadership Association, P.O. Box 380057, East Hartford, CT 06138–0057.

Purpose: To recognize by awarding scholarships to students who most nearly demonstrate the inventive genius of both Thomas Edison and Max McGraw.

Areas: Science and/or engineering.

Description: Students write a proposal which may be an abstract of an already completed experiment or a project idea which deals with a practical application in the fields of science and/or engineering.

Eligibility: Open to all students in grades 9–12.

Guidelines Availability: Contact sponsor.

Deadline: December 15.

Winner Notification: Finalists notified by February 15.

How to Enter: There is no formal entry form. The entry consists of two copies of the proposal and a letter of recommendation. The cover sheet of the proposal must contain: the title of the entry; student's name; home address; home telephone number; student's grade level; teacher/sponsor's name; name of school; school address; school telephone number; and name of the local electric utility.

Judging Criteria: Creativity and ingenuity are used as criteria.

Judges: Selected panel of judges.

Awards: The 10 finalists will present their projects before a panel of judges in efforts to select two Grand Award Scholar finalists. All expenses for transportation, lodging, and meals at the judging site, in addition to a ceremonial program, will be funded. The two finalists selected as Thomas Edison/Max McGraw Grand Award Scholars will receive $5,000 and $3,000 scholarships, respectively. The eight remaining finalists will receive $1,500 each.

Advice: All entries become the property of the Max McGraw Foundation Scholarship Program and the NSELA. Any entry not subscribing to all rules and regulations may be disqualified.

Competition: The U.S. Army's Junior Science and Humanities Symposia.

Sponsor: The Academy of Applied Science, 98 Washington St., Concord, NH 03301.

Purpose: To enhance science and engineering education from the pre–college level to undergraduate and graduate levels.

Areas: Science and engineering.

Description: Students submit a written abstract and report of scientific research.

Eligibility: Students in grades 9–12.

Important Dates: National Symposium held annually in May.

Competition Origin: 1958.

Guidelines Availability: Write to sponsor, requesting guidelines.

Deadline: Contact regional sponsor for your area.

Winner Notification: Awards presented at each symposium.

How to Enter: Individual regional symposia have specific application forms and varying application deadlines. Generally, any serious student with potential or demonstrated interest in experimental research is eligible to attend. Students in grades 9–12 are eligible. The regional symposia mail applications directly to schools and other interested organizations or individuals. Approval for a student's attendance must come from a teacher or other school official.

Judging Criteria: Quality of the research and experimentation; evidence of the student's understanding of the scientific, mathematical, or engineering principles employed in the investigation; originality and creativity; acknowledgement of major assistance; and quality of the presentation.

Judges: University scientists and educators.

Awards: Scholarships, certificates, and community recognition activities.

▼ ▽ ▼ ▽ ▼ ▽ ▼ ▽ ▼ ▽ ▼ ▽ ▼ ▽ ▼ ▽

Competition: Westinghouse Science Talent Search.

Sponsor: Science Service, 1719 N Street N.W., Washington, DC 20036.

Purpose: To foster the education of young potential scientists, mathematicians, and engineers.

Areas: Science, math, and engineering.

Description: Entering high school seniors submit a written report of an independent science, mathematics, or engineering research project.

Eligibility: Entering high school seniors.

Important Dates:

mid–August	entry materials available for request
early December	deadline for receipt of entry
mid–January	300 semi-finalists announced
late January	40 finalists announced
early March	trip to Washington, DC exhibition of projects, selection of top scholarship winners, and awards ceremony

Competition Origin: Science Service was established in 1921.

Guidelines Availability: Mid–August.

Deadline: Entries must be received in early December.

Winner Notification: In late January finalists are announced.

How to Enter: Contact sponsor for official rules and entry form.

Judging Criteria: Evidence of creativity and interest in science.

Judges: Team of more than 20 evaluators and judges specializing in a variety of scientific disciplines.

Awards: Three hundred semi-finalists benefit in the following ways: (1) recommendations to colleges and universities for admission and financial assistance; (2) certificates of achievement for students and teachers; and (3) a fine sense of accomplishment and a measure of self–esteem that come from finishing a hard assignment. The 40 finalists, selected from the semi-finalists,

△ ▲ △ ▲ △ ▲ △ ▲ △ ▲ △ ▲ △ ▲ △ ▲ △ ▲ △

are also awarded a trip to Washington, DC, for the five–day all–expenses–paid Science Talent Institute for final judging and a chance to share $205,000 in scholarships.

Advice: The research project must be the work of a single individual. Group projects are not eligible.

Environmental Science

▼ ▼ ▼ ▼ ▼ ▼ ▼ ▼ ▼ ▼ ▼ ▼ ▼ ▼

Competition: A Pledge and A Promise Environmental Awards.

Sponsor: Education Department, Sea World, 7007 Sea World Dr., Orlando, FL 32821.

Purpose: To recognize the outstanding efforts of school groups in the areas of environmental awareness and action.

Area: Environmental science.

Description: These awards are primarily service—oriented with some academics included. The awards focus on the actions school groups take to help protect the planet's natural resources.

Eligibility: All school ages are eligible to apply for these awards. They are not gender specific. The four categories are: K–5, 6–8, 9–12, and college.

Important Dates: Applications are available in September and are due by January 30.

Deadline: January 30.

Winner Notification: Winner notification occurs in the spring (date varies).

How to Enter: School groups within these categories can enter the A Pledge and A Promise Environmental Awards by submitting the environmental projects they have completed or works in progress to better the planet around them.

Judging Criteria: Several criteria are considered by the judges. They consider the projects based on their creativity, innovation, measurable effects, benefits to the community, and benefits to the environment. The judges will examine whether the projects are transferable. That is, do they serve as a model for other groups to imitate and implement. Also, they will consider whether the projects offer a long—term gain for the environment and community. Other criteria considered are that the projects be developed and implemented prior to the application deadline and that they be student—driven.

Judges: The judges for the competition are representatives from several environmental organizations. These include: Center for Marine Conservation, Hubbs–Sea World Research Institute, the Izaak Walton League of America, the National Fish and Wildlife Federation, the National Wildlife Federation, and the Sea World/Busch Gardens Education Departments.

▲ ▲ ▲ ▲ ▲ ▲ ▲ ▲ ▲ ▲ ▲ ▲ ▲ ▲

Awards: Cash awards are presented for these environmental projects. A total of 13 given across the four categories. In each age category, the following awards are presented: first place—$12,500; second place—$5,000; and third place—$2,500. A grand prize of $20,000 is awarded to the one project that is judged the overall best in any category. All awards are made on behalf of and for the advancement of the school group's project.

Advice: It is critical that the application be completed accurately and that the project is creative and student–driven.

▼ ▽ ▼ ▽ ▼ ▽ ▼ ▽ ▼ ▽ ▼ ▽ ▼ ▽ ▼ ▽

Competition: The Explorers Club Youth Activity Fund.

Sponsor: The Explorers Club Youth Activity Fund, 46 E. 70th St., New York, NY 10021.

Purpose: To help foster a new generation of explorers and to build a reservoir of young men and women dedicated to the advancement of knowledge of the world by probing the unknown through field research.

Area: Natural sciences.

Description: Grants may be requested to cover investigations anywhere in the world. Applicants must provide a brief but knowledgeable explanation of the proposed project in their own words and two letters of recommendation. The awards will be to support field work or closely related endeavors. Transportation, supplies, subsistence, and equipment are appropriate, but salaries and expenses such as tuition or indirect costs are not. Joint funding is strongly encouraged and applicants should list other sources of funds.

Grantees are expected to submit a report/essay with an itemized statement of expenses at the end of the project. Photographs are particularly encouraged. Publications based on work supported entirely or in part by The Explorers Club should credit The Explorers Club Youth Activity Fund. Copies of the publication should be forwarded to the club.

Eligibility: Grants are made to high school and college undergraduate students.

Guidelines Availability: Write to the sponsor for guidelines.

Deadline: Applications are to be submitted before the end of April.

Winner Notification: Awards are announced at the end of May.

How to Enter: Contact sponsor.

Awards: Although there is no strict limit, grants typically are in the range of several hundred to one–thousand dollars. In some cases grants will be co–funded by local chapters of The Explorers Club. Only a limited number of applicants from a single institution can expect to be funded in any year.

Advice: Projects must be carried out under supervision of a qualified scientist.

▲ ▲ ▲ ▲ ▲ ▲ ▲ ▲ ▲ ▲ ▲ ▲ ▲ ▲ ▲

Competition: Federal Junior Duck Stamp Conservation and Design Program.

Sponsor: U.S. Fish and Wildlife Service, Federal Duck Stamp Office, 1849 C St. N.W., Washington, DC 20240.

Purpose: To teach wetlands awareness and conservation through the arts to students kindergarten through high school.

Areas: Designs of North American ducks, swans, or geese in natural habitats.

Description: The JDS program is a curriculum–based art education program for kindergarten through high school students. One of the activities suggested in the curriculum guide is designing a Junior Duck Stamp — a stamp that is sold by the Wildlife service every year — and entering that design in the state JDS contest.

Eligibility: Open to all K–12 students.

Important Dates: Contact the state sponsor.

Competition Origin: 1989.

Guidelines Availability: Information is mailed to schools in October. Teachers may write to sponsor for a free curriculum guide and a JDS video.

Deadline: Varies with each state competition.

Winner Notification: November.

How to Enter: Mail your design to your state sponsor.

Judging Criteria: Accurate depiction of wildlife in its natural habitat.

Judges: Each state selects five judges.

Awards: The U.S. Fish and Wildlife Service awards a certificate of participation to each student who enters a design, 100 ribbons across all age categories, and a State Best of Show ribbon. In some states, sponsors may offer additional prizes. The national first, second, and third place winners, their art teachers, and one of their parents win a free trip to Washington, DC, to attend the Federal Duck Stamp Contest. The first place winner also receives a $2,500 award.

▼ ▼ ▼ ▼ ▼ ▼ ▼ ▼ ▼ ▼ ▼ ▼ ▼

Competition: Firestone Firehawks.

Sponsor: Bridgestone/Firestone Inc., 50 Century Blvd., Nashville, TN 37219.

Purpose: To recognize children between the ages of 5 and 15 for their efforts on behalf of the environment.

Area: Environmental advocacy.

Description: Children are inducted into the Firehawks club (receive T–shirts and other memorabilia), and have the opportunity to win an all–expenses–paid trip to Olympic National Park in Washington.

Eligibility: All children, 5 to 15 years old.

Important Dates: The trip is scheduled for July each year.

Competition Origin: 1991.

Guidelines Availability: Requests for applications are accepted year–round. Application forms are printed in January and are sent to all who have made requests since the last contest.

Deadline: Mid–April.

Winner Notification: Mid–May.

How to Enter: The application form requires vital information as well as supporting information about the environmental program.

Judging Criteria: Activity versus age abilities, the number of people served by the activity, and the duration of the activity.

Judges: Bridgestone/Firestone and an independent panel of judges are selected each year.

Awards: Club memorabilia, all–expenses–paid excursion to Olympic National Park for Environmental Education.

▲ ▲ ▲ ▲ ▲ ▲ ▲ ▲ ▲ ▲ ▲ ▲ ▲

Competition: President's Environmental Youth Awards.

Sponsor: U.S. Environmental Protection Agency, 401 M St. S.W., Washington, DC 20104.

Purpose: To offer young people an opportunity to become an environmental force within their community.

Areas: Environmental issues and service.

Description: The program has two components: the regional certificate program and the national awards competition. Students are recognized for their efforts to make and keep the world around us a safer, cleaner place to live.

Eligibility: Open to all age groups. Students may compete as individuals, school classes, schools, summer camps, public interest groups, and youth organizations.

Important Dates: Regional applications are accepted year round; however, at the national level, applications must be submitted by July 31.

Guidelines Availability: Contact your regional EPA office for guidelines which are available year–round.

Deadline: July 31.

How to Enter: Obtain an application and detailed guidelines from your regional EPA office.

Judging Criteria: The judging panel considers the following:
*   Environmental need for the project;
*   Environmental appropriateness of the project;
*   Accomplishment of goals;
*   Long–term environmental benefits derived from the project;
*   Positive environmental impact on the local community and society;
*   Evidence of the young person's initiative;
*   Innovation;
*   Soundness of approach, rationale, and scientific design (if applicable); and
*   Clarity and effectiveness of presentation.

Judges: Judging panel selected by the EPA.

Awards: All participants at the regional level receive certificates signed by the president of the United States, honoring them for their efforts in environmental protection. The national winners, along with one project sponsor, receive an all–expenses–paid trip to Washington, DC, where they participate in the annual National Awards Ceremony and consult with the EPA Youth Work Group about the program. They also receive a $1,000 grant from Keebler Company. Church & Dwight Company Inc., makers of Arm & Hammer Baking Soda, hosts a luncheon and presents an additional $1,000 grant to each winner, as well as a smaller grant to the first, second, and third place runners–up in each region.

Advice: Contact your regional EPA office.

General Science

Competition: American Junior Academy of Science.

Sponsor: National Association of Academics of Science, 900 Exposition Blvd., Los Angeles, CA 90007.

Purpose: To introduce, encourage, and accelerate high school students into the world of science, engineering, and technology.

Area: Science.

Description: Students conduct research in science and are chosen to be delegates to the annual meeting of the American Association for the Advancement of Science by their State Academy of Science, State Junior Academy of Science, or a comparable organization.

Eligibility: Open to all high school students.

Important Dates: The annual meeting of the American Association for the Advancement of Science is held in February of each year.

Guidelines Availability: Contact the sponsor for a brochure. Your state academies' office should have registration and program information available in July, October, and January.

How to Enter: Contact your state academy.

Judging Criteria: Students are selected based upon the quality of research and the ability to communicate through written and oral presentations.

Awards: Students are invited to annual meetings of the American Association for the Advancement of Science.

Advice: Students must seek a sponsor or raise money to cover registration fees, meals, travel, and lodging at the annual meeting.

Competition: DuPont Challenge Science Essay Awards Program.

Sponsor: General Learning Corporation, 60 Revere Dr., Northbrook, IL 60062–1563.

Purpose: To promote student interest in all avenues of science.

Areas: Anthropology, archaeology, astronomy, biology, biochemistry, biomedical sciences, biotechnology, chemistry, computer sciences, engineering, environmental sciences, genetics, geology, geophysics, mathematics, medicine, paleontology, and physics.

Description: The DuPont Challenge for students is to write an essay of 700 to 1,000 words discussing a scientific development, event, or theory that has captured your interest and attention.

Eligibility: A student must be regularly and currently enrolled in grades 7 through 12 in a public or non–public school in the United States and its territories or Canada.

Important Dates: Entries may be submitted beginning in October.

Guidelines Availability: Contact the sponsor for guidelines.

Deadline: January.

Judging Criteria: An appropriate choice of subject matter, thorough research using a variety of resource materials, careful consideration of how the subject matter affects you and humankind, a clear, well–organized writing style that has been proofed for spelling and grammatical errors.

Awards: Winners of the DuPont Challenge Science Essay Awards Program receive national recognition and a significant financial grant. The program, sponsored by DuPont in cooperation with General Learning Corporation and the National Science Teachers Association, awards cash prizes totaling nearly $8,000.

Three winners and 24 honorable mentions are awarded in each of two divisions: junior division (grades 7, 8, and 9) and senior division (grades 10, 11, and 12).

Competition: Egg Loft.

Sponsor: Estes Industries and National Science Olympiad, Educational Services, Estes Industries, 1295 H St., P.O. Box 227, Penrose, CO 81240.

Purpose: To safely launch and recover a fragile payload (egg–astronaut) without damaging it.

Areas: Science, physics, math, and industrial technology.

Description: The Egg Loft competition is comprised of a single–staged model rocket that carries, as a totally enclosed payload, one raw medium hen's egg. The purpose of this competition is to carry an exceedingly fragile payload for as long a time as possible and to recover the payload without damage.

Eligibility: Entrant must be a National Science Olympiad participant; Junior High and High School Divisions.

Important Dates: Regional competitions are held in March, state competitions in April, and national competitions in May.

Guidelines Availability: Through Estes Industries and the National Science Olympiad.

Deadline: Contact National Science Olympiad for deadlines.

Winner Notification: Winners are announced at the national competition.

How to Enter: A school enters a team in the Science Olympiad and competes at the national level.

Judging Criteria: Judged based upon pre–flight safety check, post–flight condition of payload, launch equipment and engine, weather, and timing.

Judges: Volunteers at regional and state levels, Estes Industries staff at national level.

Awards: Medals are given at the national competition.

Competition: International Science and Engineering Fair.

Sponsor: Science Service Inc., 1719 N Street N.W., Washington, DC 20036.

Purpose: To promote science and education by providing formalized structure for over 400 affiliated science fairs.

Areas: Behavioral and social science, botany, computer science, engineering, mathematics, microbiology, zoology, biochemistry, chemistry, earth and space sciences, environmental sciences, medicine and health, physics, and team projects.

Description: Students advance from local, regional, state, and national science fairs to compete at the ISEF.

Eligibility: Each ISEF affiliated fair may send up to two finalists and one team project to the ISEF. Any student in grades 9–12 or equivalent is eligible, none of whom has reached age 21 on or before May 1 preceding the ISEF.

Important Dates: Contact sponsor for dates.

Competition Origin: 1950.

Guidelines Availability: Contact your local science fair coordinator or the sponsor for details.

Deadline: Varies year to year, usually late spring.

Winner Notification: Winners are notified at the conclusion of each fair.

How to Enter: Complete application and forms as distributed by the sponsor.

Judging Criteria: Vary with each level of competition.

Judges: International experts from the fields of science, mathematics, and engineering.

Awards: Winners earn grand awards and special awards. From the grand award winners, two students are selected each year to receive all–expenses–paid trips to the Nobel Prize ceremonies held in Stockholm, Sweden. The two Glenn Seaborg Nobel Prize First Award winners participate in activities of the Stockholm International Youth Science Seminar while in Stockholm. The top team projects will attend the European Community Contest for Young Scientists.

Competition: National Science Olympiad.

Sponsor: National Science Olympiad, Box 2196, St. James, NY 11780.

Purpose: To improve science skills.

Areas: Life science, general science, earth science, chemistry, physics, and biology.

Description: A 50–question test is administered to participants in late April/early May.

Eligibility: Open to all students in grades 2–12.

Important Dates: Register by February 10. Test administered in late April/early May.

Competition Origin: 1982.

Guidelines Availability: Available from sponsor in May.

Deadline: February 10.

Winner Notification: Winners are notified in May.

How to Enter: Register by mail to sponsor's address.

Awards: Medals and certificates are awarded to winners.

Competition: Science Olympiad.

Sponsor: Science Olympiad, 704 N. Bradford St., Dover, DE 19904 or Science Olympiad, 5955 Little Pine Lane, Rochester Hills, MI 48306.

Purpose: To challenge students to reach for higher goals and aspirations — to be all that they can be; to increase the interest of pre–college students in science, mathematics, and technology such that high–tech careers are an option as the students matriculate into institutions of higher education; and to wrap these serious intents into a context of a fun, exciting activity.

Areas: Science, mathematics, and technology.

Description: The Science Olympiad is an international non–profit organization devoted to improving the quality of science education, increasing student interest in science, and providing recognition for outstanding achievement in science education by both students and teachers. These goals are accomplished through classroom activities, research, training workshops, and the encouragement of intramural, district, regional, state, and national tournaments. The Science Olympiad tournaments are rigorous academic, inter-scholastic competitions that consist of a series of 32 individual and team events which students prepare for during the year. The competitions follow the format of popular board games, TV shows, and athletic games. These challenging and motivational events are balanced between the disciplines of biology, earth science, chemistry, physics, computers, and technology. There is also a balance between events requiring knowledge of science facts, concepts, processes, skills, and applications. In addition, during the day there are open house activities which consist of science and mathematics demonstrations, activities, and career counseling sessions conducted by professors and scientists at the host institution occurring concurrently with the events. Many states and regions have organized physics, biology, or chemistry Olympiads, but few have combined all disciplines in one large Olympiad. The excitement of many students from all science areas competing and cheering one another on to greater learning caused one school district to coin the phrase "intellete." When they searched for a place to house their newly won Olympiad State Championship trophy, the only location available was outside the principal's office in the "athlete" showcase, so they convinced the school board to build an "intellete" showcase. An intellete is any person who demonstrates outstanding performance in an academic or intellectual pursuit (in this case, science). One of the goals of the Science Olympiad is to elevate science education and learning to a level of enthusiasm and support that is normally reserved only for varsity sports programs.

▼ ▽ ▼ ▽ ▼ ▽ ▼ ▽ ▼ ▽ ▼ ▽ ▼ ▽ ▼

Eligibility: The Olympiad has four divisions as noted below. Only Divisions B and C have state, regional, and national competitions. Division A (A1 or A2) has only local or district activities.

Division	Grade Levels
A1	K–3
A2	3–6
B	6–9
C	9–12

Important Dates: Each local, county, district, and state sets its own dates for competitions. The National Tournament is generally held during the third weekend in May. Since attendance at the National Tournament requires placement at state tournaments, states generally hold their competitions no later than mid–April.

Competition Origin: 1984.

Guidelines Availability: Rules Manual and Coaches Guide are available from the national offices.

Deadline: Deadlines vary by state and region.

Winner Notification: All participants are assembled at the tournament site at the end of the day. At all tournaments an awards ceremony is held and winners are named.

How to Enter: Contact the national office for advice on registering.

Judging Criteria: Judging criteria vary from event to event but are defined in the Rules Manual available from the national office.

Judges: Each tournament site is responsible for finding local judges with the technical expertise to judge the activity. This is the reason that many tournaments are held at college or university sites.

Awards: Trophies are given to schools, winning coaches get plaques, and students receive Olympic–style medals.

▲ ▲ ▲ ▲ ▲ ▲ ▲ ▲ ▲ ▲ ▲ ▲ ▲ ▲ ▲

Competition: TEAMS (Tests of Engineering Aptitude, Mathematics, and Science).

Sponsor: Junior Engineering Technical Society Inc. (JETS), 1420 King St., Suite 405, Alexandria, VA 22314–2794.

Purpose: To enable teams of high school students to learn team development and problem–solving skills.

Areas: Mathematics and science.

Description: Teams participate in an open–book, open–discussion environment to solve real–world engineering problems. Teams learn how the mathematics and science concepts they are learning in high school are applied to real–world problems. TEAMS problems focus on all areas of mathematics and science, as well as on computer fundamentals, graphics interpretation, and English/communication skills and concepts.

Eligibility: All students in grades 9 through 12 may participate. Teams are made up of between four and eight members. Varsity and Junior Varsity division are available at most sites.

Important Dates: TEAMS is a one–day, two–part event held between early February and mid–March each year. Schools may begin registering teams beginning in September.

Competition Origin: TEAMS was established in 1979.

Guidelines Availability: Information is updated each summer for the following year's TEAMS program. Schools or students may request information year–round.

Deadline: The deadline for registering for TEAMS varies by site, but generally is about one month before the competition date. All registered schools receive coaching and practice materials, so the earlier schools register, the more time they will have to prepare.

Winner Notification: Teams usually receive local (regional) results on competition day. State rankings are announced one week after the last competition date. National rankings are announced by mid–April.

How to Enter: Schools that have not participated before should contact JETS for information on the competition site nearest them. All schools register directly with the competition host.

Judging Criteria: TEAMS consists of a two–part exam. Part 1 is multiple–choice and is scored on competition day. Part 1 determines both regional and state rankings. Top–scoring teams in each of nine Varsity and nine Junior Varsity divisions in each state are eligible for national ranking, which is based on part 2, the subjective portion of the exam. Part 2 is scored by a panel of engineers determined by JETS and the TEAMS problem development coordinator.

Awards: Awards are given for regional, state, and national recognition. Regional and state awards vary by site and state. National awards are given by JETS and vary from year to year.

Advice: Register early in order to receive coaching and preparation materials in time to make them useful.

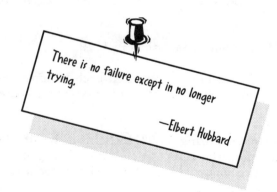

There is no failure except in no longer trying.

—Elbert Hubbard

Competition: The Thomas Edison/Max McGraw Scholarship Program.

Sponsor: Edison/McGraw Scholarship Program, National Science Education Leadership Association, P.O. Box 380057, East Hartford, CT 06138–0057.

Purpose: To recognize by awarding scholarships to students who most nearly demonstrate the inventive genius of both Thomas Edison and Max McGraw.

Areas: Science and/or engineering.

Description: Students write a proposal which may be an abstract of an already complete experiment or a project idea which deals with a practical application in the fields of science and/or engineering.

Eligibility: Open to all students in grades 9–12.

Important Dates: Entries must be postmarked no later than December 15.

Guidelines Availability: Contact sponsor.

Deadline: December 15.

Winner Notification: Finalists are notified by February 15.

How to Enter: There is no formal entry form. The entry consists of two copies of the proposal and a letter of recommendation. The cover sheet of the proposal must contain: the title of the entry; student's name; home address; home telephone number; student's grade level; teacher/sponsor's name; name of school; school address; school telephone number; and name of the local electric utility.

Judging Criteria: Creativity and ingenuity are used as criteria.

Awards: The ten finalists will present their projects before a panel of judges in efforts to select two Grand Award Scholar finalists. All expenses for transportation, lodging, and meals at the judging site, in addition to a ceremonial program, will be funded. The two finalists selected as Thomas Edison/Max McGraw Grand Award Scholars will receive $5,000 and $3,000 scholarships, respectively. The eight remaining finalists will receive $1,500 each.

Advice: All entries become the property of the Max McGraw Foundation Scholarship Program and the NSELA. Any entry not subscribing to all rules and regulations may be disqualified.

Competition: Westinghouse Science Talent Search.

Sponsor: Science Service, 1719 N St. N.W., Washington, DC 20036.

Purpose: To foster the education of young potential scientists, mathematicians, and engineers.

Areas: Science, math, and engineering.

Description: Entering high school seniors submit a written report of an independent science, mathematics, or engineering research project.

Eligibility: Open to all entering high school seniors.

Important Dates:

mid–August	entry materials available for request
early December	deadline for receipt of entry
mid–January	300 semi-finalists announced
late January	40 finalists announced
early March	trip to Washington, DC exhibition of projects, selection of top scholarship winners, and awards ceremony

Competition Origin: Science Service was established in 1921.

Guidelines Availability: Available from the sponsor in mid–August.

Deadline: Early December.

Winner Notification: Finalists are announced in late January.

How to Enter: Contact sponsor for official rules and entry form.

Judging Criteria: Evidence of creativity and interest in science.

Judges: Team of more than 20 evaluators and judges specializing in a variety of scientific disciplines.

Awards: Three hundred semi-finalists benefit in the following ways: (1) recommendations to colleges and universities for admission and financial assistance; (2) certificates of achievement for students and teachers; and (3) a fine sense of accomplishment and a measure of self–esteem that come from finishing a hard assignment. The 40 finalists, selected from the semi-finalists, are also awarded a trip to Washington, DC, for the five–day all–expenses–paid Science Talent Institute for final judging and a chance to share $205,000 in scholarships.

Advice: The research project must be the work of a single individual. Group projects are not eligible.

Inventions and Games

Competition: Duracell/NSTA Scholarship Competition.

Sponsor: Duracell NSTA Scholarship Competition, 1840 Wilson Blvd., Arlington, VA 22201–3000.

Purpose: To design and build working devices powered by Duracell batteries.

Areas: Inventions.

Description: Participants submit ideas for devices, with description, wiring diagram/schematic, and photograph. The top 100 finalists are notified to send the actual device for judging.

Eligibility: Students in grades 9–12 residing in the United States or U.S. Territories.

Important Dates: Mid–November for idea submission.

Guidelines Availability: Year–round.

Deadline: Competition entry deadline is mid–January. Ideas must be received by mid–November.

Winner Notification: The top six winners will be notified at the NSTA National Convention Awards Banquet.

How to Enter: Write or call Duracell/NSTA Scholarship Competition.

Awards: Winners receive the following: one first place award of $20,000; five second place awards of $10,000; 10 third place awards of $1,000; 25 fourth place awards of $500; 59 fifth place awards of $100. The top six winners, their parents, and teacher/sponsors will be flown to the site of the NSTA National convention to attend an awards banquet held in the winners' honor. Teachers of the six top winners will receive personal computers. Ten third place teachers receive a $50 gift certificate for NSTA Publications. Twenty–five fourth place teachers receive Duracell Gifts. Personalized Award Certificates are given for the top 100 finalists. Everyone who enters will receive a gift and a certificate.

Competition: ERECTOR Challenge.

Sponsor: The ERECTOR Set Company, 1675 Broadway, 31st Floor, New York, NY 10019; Attn: Educational Programs Department.

Purpose: To challenge students in an interactive environment to learn about the history of a topic and to explore its future.

Areas: Inventing.

Description: Class utilizes learning materials about a certain topic. Then they design their own "future" car, spaceship, or whatever the topic is and write an essay to be sent to ERECTOR. Twenty classes are selected as finalists. To each finalist, four of the largest ERECTOR Sets are sent so that each can bring its design "to life." Each class submits a photo. Ten are selected as winners. This program is offered free.

Eligibility: Open to all students 8 years of age and older.

Important Dates: Program is run in the spring (January through April/May) and fall (October through December). Teachers should send in postcard in order to be put into the database and receive information about the year's topic.

Competition Origin: In 1916 the inventor of the ERECTOR Sets held the first nationwide building contest. For the toy's 80th anniversary, the company brought these contests back to life.

Deadline: Teachers are sent a timeline to determine if it will fit in the curricula.

Winner Notification: Winners receive phone calls and letters.

How to Enter: Send a postcard to ERECTOR Challenge.

Judging Criteria: Submissions that demonstrate an understanding of the topic as well as creativity. Each grade is judged by skill level.

Judges: Experts related to the topic from outside of the company.

Awards: Every child who participates as part of a class receives a certificate. Winning classes receive a monetary award and a plaque.

Advice: Be prepared to put in a lot of "hands on" time. Be sure to discuss this with your teacher in the early fall.

Competition: Fire Fighting Home Robot Contest.

Sponsor: Trinity College and Connecticut Robotics Society, 190 Mohegan Dr., West Hartford, CT 06117.

Purpose: To build a computer–controlled robot that can find and extinguish a fire in a house.

Areas: Robotics.

Description: Students of all ages build real computer-controlled, programmed robots that perform a necessary function in the home.

Eligibility: Open to anyone of any age or ability. The contest is open to groups or individuals.

Important Dates: This annual competition is held in late spring.

Competition Origin: Began in 1994 as an outgrowth of educational programs run by the Connecticut Robotics Society.

Guidelines Availability: Contact the Connecticut Robotics Society.

Deadlines: The deadline for entry is 30 days before the contest date which changes each year.

Winner Notification: All prizes are awarded at the competition.

How to Enter: Contact the sponsor.

Judging Criteria: The capability of the robot to quickly find and extinguish a fire in a house.

Awards: $1,000 first place and additional prizes for second–10th places.

Advice: Get the rules and start working early.

Competition: *SuperScience Blue*'s Annual Toy Tester Contest.

Sponsor: *SuperScience Blue*, Scholastic, 555 Broadway, New York, NY 10012–3999.

Purpose: To allow students the opportunity to put their hands–on science skills to a competitive test.

Areas: Toy testing.

Description: Participants take a simple toy of the sponsor's design and improve its performance.

Eligibility: Open to all students in grades 4–6. Participants can work in teams of up to five.

Important Dates: Contest deadline is in late December.

Competition Origin: 1990.

Guidelines Availability: A Super Foldout which includes guidelines comes with each set of *SuperScience Blue*'s November/December issue.

Deadline: Late December.

Winner Notification: Winners are notified by March and announced in the May issue.

How to Enter: Follow details as described in the November/December fold-out.

Judging Criteria: Entries are judged according to performance (80 percent), creativity (10 percent), and lab report (10 percent).

Judges: *SuperScience Blue*'s staff.

Awards: Science toys and books for winning student teams and catalog gift certificates to their teachers.

▼ ▼ ▼ ▼ ▼ ▼ ▼ ▼ ▼ ▼ ▼ ▼ ▼ ▼ ▼

Competition: Young Inventors and Creators Program.

Sponsor: National Inventive Thinking Association, P.O. Box 836202, Richardson, TX 75083.

Purpose: To recognize creative and inventive thinking skills.

Areas: YOUNG INVENTORS PATENT CATEGORIES: Health Invention, Invention for Business/Office Use, Household/Food Invention, Agricultural Invention, Invention for New Technology, Leisure Time/Entertainment Invention, Environmental Invention.

YOUNG CREATORS COPYRIGHT CATEGORIES: Short Story, Poem, Classical Musical Composition, Popular Musical Composition, Dramatic Work/Video, Painting/Graphic.

Description: The Young Inventors and Creators Program goal is to encourage students' and teachers' interest in the governmental systems that encourage and protect the creative processes leading to societal benefits and a range of professional opportunities.

Eligibility: Grades 7–12.

Important Dates: Mid–June to mid–August: Judging at the state level takes place.

August 31: State judging will be completed and entries sent to the Patent and Trademark Office and Copyright Office.

September 1: National finalists will be evaluated by two teams; a creative arts team assembled by the U.S. Copyright Office, and an invention team assembled by the U.S. Patent and Trademark Office.

Late September: Students to receive national recognition and their teachers will be notified.

October: National winners will be appropriately recognized at the National Creative and Inventive Thinking Skills Conference.

Competition Origin: 1986.

Guidelines Availability: Contact the sponsor or your state/regional representative.

▲ ▲ ▲ ▲ ▲ ▲ ▲ ▲ ▲ ▲ ▲ ▲ ▲ ▲ ▲

Deadline: Mid–June submission date for all state and regional entries.

Winner Notification: By mail during summer or fall months.

How to Enter: Entries must include the title of the invention, a written explanation of what it is for, how it works, how you got your idea, accompanying drawings, photographs or videotapes that best illustrates your invention. Submission must be made on 8½" x 11" papers; all narratives must be typed. Models must not be submitted but may be required if your entry becomes a national finalist. You may submit entries in more than one category. Each individual entry requires a separate entry form. You may not submit more than one entry per form. Entries must fall into one of the eight invention categories listed in the general rules and be so marked on the entry form.

Judging Criteria: Young Inventor: Originality or novelty (How unique or new is it?); usefulness (Does it solve a problem? How marketable is it?); drawing, photograph, or videotape of the invention (complete with all parts labeled); and written description (content, legibility, clarity of expression). Young Creator: Creativity (60 percent); originality of idea, content, thematic relevance; presentation (40 percent); clarity of expression, and effective use of form or medium.

Judges: U.S. Copyright and U.S. Patent and Trademark Office teams.

Awards: All students reaching the regional or state level will get certificates of participation, winners at the state or regional levels will receive certificates of achievement, and the national winners will be recognized at the National Creative and Inventive Thinking Skills Conference.

▼ ▼ ▼ ▼ ▼ ▼ ▼ ▼ ▼ ▼ ▼ ▼ ▼ ▼ ▼

Competition: Young Game Inventors Contest.

Sponsor: U.S. Kids, P.O. Box 567, Indianapolis, IN 46206.

Purpose: To provide students an opportunity to apply their creativity in inventing a board game.

Areas: Inventing.

Description: Students ages 13 and under create an original board game, including rules and game board.

Eligibility: Children no more than 13 years of age.

Important Dates: Entries must be postmarked June 30.

Competition Origin: 1993.

Guidelines Availability: Contact sponsor.

Deadline: Entries must bear a June 30 postmark.

How to Enter: Submit game and entrance form to sponsor.

Judging Criteria: Judges look for a fun game and a creative idea.

Judges: University Games Officials.

Awards: All participants will receive a 1995 Young Game Inventors certificate and seal of achievement. Four first–prize winners will receive an assortment of University Games' toys and games, including autographed copies of Joshua White's Dinomite game and Derek Nelson's Take a Hike game; and a two–year subscription to one of Children's Better Health Institute's (CBHI) seven magazines: U.S. Kids, Jack and Jill, Child Life, Children's Digest, Humpty Dumpty Magazine, Turtle, or Children's Playmate. The grand–prize winner will receive an expense–paid trip for three to San Francisco (four nights lodging, rental car use, and airfare); the chance to have his or her game manufactured by University Games; a $200 shopping spree at the Imaginarium; an assortment of University Games' toys and games, including autographed copies of Joshua White's Dinomite game and Derek Nelson's Take a Hike game; a two–year subscription to one of CBHI's seven magazines; a tour of San Francisco and University Games; a special party; and his or her name and picture in four of CBHI's magazines.

▲ ▲ ▲ ▲ ▲ ▲ ▲ ▲ ▲ ▲ ▲ ▲ ▲ ▲ ▲

Physics

Competition: Physics Bowl.

Sponsor: American Association of Physics Teachers, One Physics Ellipse, College Park, MD 20740–3845.

Purpose: To encourage interest in physics and recognize students' scientific achievement and excellence in teaching.

Area: Physics.

Description: All students who enter take a 40–question, timed, multiple–choice test supervised at their school. Contest questions are based on topics and concepts in typical high school physics courses.

Eligibility: The contest is designed to be challenging. First and second year physics students will compete in separate divisions. Division I is for first year students. Division II is for second year students. In each region, students will compete in one of the two divisions. A school may enter either or both divisions as long as it has at least four eligible students. A school's score in a division is the sum of the four highest student scores. Specialized science and math high schools compete in a separate region. Physics formulas are provided.

Guidelines Availability: Ongoing.

Deadline: The end of March.

How to Enter: Request application materials.

Judging Criteria: Objective test answers.

Awards: All first–place schools will receive a laser donated by Metrologic. First and second–place teams will also receive T–shirts. All students and teachers who enter the Physics Bowl will receive a certificate of participation from the AAPT.

Don't be influenced by what others are
doing—stick with your way and do your
best.

—12-year-old girl

Space and Astronomy

▼ ▾ ▼ ▾ ▼ ▾ ▼ ▾ ▼ ▾ ▼ ▾ ▼ ▾ ▼ ▾

Competition: National Outstanding Young Astronomer Award.

Sponsor: The Astronomical League, c/o Vice–President, NOYAA, 1007 Rollingwood Lane, Goshen, KY 40026.

Purpose: To recognize outstanding achievement in astronomy by high school aged amateur astronomers.

Area: Astronomy.

Description: A national panel of judges selects the winner based upon the student's overall achievements in astronomy. Activities which the judges consider include astronomical research, astronomical articles published, local astronomical club activities, academic achievements in science and math, involvement in regional and national astronomy organizations, observing history and skills, astrophotography and/or CCD Imaging, public education experience, and telescope design.

Eligibility: The competition is open to all students who are either enrolled in high school by the application deadline or who are 14 to 19 years of age and not enrolled in college on the application deadline and who are residents of the United States, its territories, or possessions.

Important Dates: The deadline for submission is January 30.

Competition Origin: 1993.

Guidelines Availability: Available year–round from sponsor.

Deadline: The end of January.

Winner Notification: Winners are notified in mid–March.

How to Enter: Fill out the application form and obtain a sponsor's signature. Prepare a typewritten summary of your achievements in astronomy, enclosing optional exhibits. Mail the application form, summary, and exhibits to the Award Chair by the award deadline (postmark date).

Judging Criteria: Award selections are, by their very nature, subjective. Accordingly, the league warrants only that awards will be presented to individuals who, in the opinion of the national judges, merit the awards. Because of staffing constraints and difficulties inherent in the award process, the Award Chair may extend deadlines or respond to special needs and circum-

▲ ^ ▲ ^ ▲ ^ ▲ ^ ▲ ^ ▲ ^ ▲ ^ ▲ ^ ▲ ^

stances in administering the award. The decisions of the national judges are final. Judges who know any applicant are required to disqualify themselves. Judges' rankings are averaged using Zip's Law (3rd place vote equals ⅓ point, fourth place vote equals ¼ point etc.). Ties are broken by the lowest total of raw rankings.

Judges: The NOYAA committee selects a national panel of judges consisting of well–known amateur and professional astronomers who review all application packages and select 10 finalists. Currently all judges are professional physicists and astronomers.

Awards: First, second, and third place winners will receive large engraved plaques. These plaques will be formally presented at the league's national convention held each summer. Alternatively, the first place award will be presented at the winner's high school awards day program or at a local astronomy organization function of the winner's choice.

▼ ▽ ▼ ▽ ▼ ▽ ▼ ▽ ▼ ▽ ▼ ▽ ▼ ▽ ▼ ▽ ▼ ▽

Competition: Space Science Student Involvement Program (SSIP).

Sponsor: National Science Teachers Association, 1840 Wilson Blvd., Arlington, VA 22201.

Purpose: To encourage students to become involved in the hands–on educational experience of space science competitions.

Area: Space science.

Description: Competitions include: The Future Aircraft/Spacecraft Design (grades 3–5); Mission to Planet Earth Team Project (grades 6–8); Mars Scientific Experiment Proposal (grades 9–12); Aerospace Internships (grades 9–12); and Interplanetary Art Competition (grades 9–12).

Eligibility: Open to all students in grades 3–12.

Important Dates: Contact sponsor for information on each competition, as dates vary.

Competition Origin: 1980.

Guidelines Availability: Write to the sponsor. Be sure to ask for information on a specific competition.

Deadline: Contact sponsor for information early in the school year.

Winner Notification: Mid–April.

How to Enter: See guidelines.

Judging Criteria: Vary with each competition.

Judges: Selected by NSTA and NASA.

Awards: Students and teachers can win trips to various NASA centers, internships with NASA scientists, space camp scholarships, medals, ribbons, certificates, and national recognition.

▲ ▲ ▲ ▲ ▲ ▲ ▲ ▲ ▲ ▲ ▲ ▲ ▲ ▲ ▲ ▲ ▲

Social Studies

Civics and Government

▼ ▼ ▼ ▼ ▼ ▼ ▼ ▼ ▼ ▼ ▼ ▼ ▼

Competition: Civic Oration Contest.

Sponsor: Fraternal Department–Youth Division, Modern Woodmen of America, 1701 First Ave., Rock Island, IL 61201.

Purpose: To encourage appreciation of citizenship in America's youth.

Areas: Speeches at local, district, state/regional, and national levels.

Description: This contest offers students an opportunity to develop their skills in clear thinking and speaking whether the student is from a school with small or large enrollment. It also provides experience in an activity of value in personal, academic, and community life. The subject is always of a positive nature. This helps to form a positive approach in preparing the speech. It also enables the student to take pride in personal accomplishments as well as pride in his or her community and America.

Eligibility: Any student in grades five through eight is eligible to compete. However, in order to be eligible for materials to be sent, a minimum of 12 students in each school must participate to be considered a Modern Woodmen of America contest.

Important Dates: May 1 and May 20 are dates for final registration for the district and regional contests. Taping for national office must be received by July.

Competition Origin: Began in 1948 as a community service.

Guidelines Availability: Fall of each year.

Deadline: Varies with level of competition.

Winner Notification: On site for local, district, and state/regional. All judgment at the national level is completed by July 20.

How to Enter: Contact your local or state Modern Woodmen representative.

Judging Criteria: Contest rules change for each level of competition.

Judges: Modern Woodmen of America representatives.

Awards: Trophies and awards vary with each level of competition, but include plaques, trophies, and saving bonds.

▲ ▲ ▲ ▲ ▲ ▲ ▲ ▲ ▲ ▲ ▲ ▲ ▲

Competition: Joseph S. Rumbaugh Oration Contest.

Sponsor: The National Society of the Sons of the American Revolution, 1000 S. Fourth St., Louisville, KY 40203.

Purpose: To bring American history to the high school student and focus on events of today; to draw an intelligent relationship between the past and the present; to clearly demonstrate freedom of opportunity as a basic right of our national heritage; to place a positive emphasis on the plans of our founding fathers; to emphasize justice under law in the free society; and to illustrate how the Revolutionary War influenced our freedom of expression which originated in the famous 1735 trial of the Colonial New York printer, John Peter Zenger.

Area: American history.

Eligibility: Open to all high school students.

Important Dates: Dates vary with level of competition.

Competition Origin: 1945.

Guidelines Availability: Contact your state society or the national office.

Winner Notification: National winners are recognized at the annual Congress on the National Society of the Sons of the American Revolution.

How to Enter: Participate at the local, state, and district levels.

Judging Criteria: Composition, delivery, logic, significance, general excellence, and time allocated for delivery are selected criteria.

Judges: Members of the Sons of the American Revolution.

Awards: Winners receive scholarship awards of first place $2,000, second place $1,000, and third place $500. All other national contestants may win $100.

Advice: Contact state sponsor early in the school year.

Competition: Freedoms Foundation National Awards Program.

Sponsor: Freedoms Foundation at Valley Forge, Rt. 23, Valley Forge, PA 19482–0706.

Purpose: To publicly honor and recognize the exceptional efforts of individuals, organizations, corporations, and schools who promote, through words or deeds, an understanding of responsible citizenship and the benefits of a free society.

Areas: Most youth category entries are in the form of written essays and speeches. However, projects for individual achievement or involvement in communities are also welcome.

Description: Eligible material must have been written, developed, or released during the May 1 to May 1 awards year.

Eligibility: Open to all citizens and legal residents of the U.S. grade K–12.

Important Dates: May 1 is deadline for entry. Award ceremonies are conducted by regional volunteer chapters beginning October 15.

Competition Origin: 1949.

Guidelines Availability: Year–round.

Deadline: May 1 of each year.

Winner Notification: Awardees will be announced by September 1 of each year.

How to Enter: Submit typed copy of essay or speech. Activities should be put in a ring binder or scrap book with substantiating materials.

Judging Criteria: A nomination must relate to one or more of the basic American rights set forth in the *American Credo* or the obligations outlined in the *Bill of Responsibilities*, both of which are Freedom Foundation documents available from the sponsor.

Judges: National Awards Jury is comprised of chief and associate State Supreme Court justices, executive offices from National Veteran Service and civic clubs, veterans, or educational organizations.

Awards: Top recipient in Youth Category receives $100 U.S. Saving Bond and framed George Washington Honor Medal. All other recipients receive a George Washington Honor Medal.

Advice: Winning entries from other local/national contests are eligible. Entries may not be the product of classroom assignments.

▼ ▽ ▼ ▽ ▼ ▽ ▼ ▽ ▼ ▽ ▼ ▽ ▼ ▽ ▼ ▽

Competition: National Peace Essay Contest.

Sponsor: United States Institute of Peace, 1550 M St. N.W., Suite 700, Washington, DC 20005.

Purpose: To promote serious discussion among high school students, teachers, and national leaders about international peace and conflict resolution, complement existing curricula; and strengthen students' research, writing, and reasoning skills.

Areas: Writing and civic education.

Description: Students write an essay on the chosen topic which may focus on topics such as international affairs, conflict resolution, social studies, history, or politics.

Eligibility: Open to U.S. citizens in grades 9-12, including those attending a high school correspondence program or an American school overseas.

Important Dates: The deadline for entry is early February.

Competition Origin: In the belief that questions about peace, justice, freedom, and security are vital to civic education, the competition was established to expand educational opportunities.

Guidelines Availability: Contact the sponsor in the fall.

Deadline: Early February.

Winner Notification: Winners are notified in May.

How to Enter: Students submit a 1,500 word essay on the chosen topic. Three copies are sent to the sponsor with an application form.

Judging Criteria: Each aspect of the given topic must be addressed. Entries are judged for their research, analysis, and form.

Awards: One winner from each state receives a $750 scholarship and a trip to Washington, DC. These winners compete for national prizes of $5,000, $2,500, and $1,000.

▲ ^ ▲ ^ ▲ ^ ▲ ^ ▲ ^ ▲ ^ ▲ ^ ▲ ^ ▲ ^ ▲ ^ ▲

Competition: National Society Daughters of the American Revolution Good Citizens Contest.

Sponsor: National Society Daughters of the American Revolution, 1776 D St. N.W., Washington, DC 20006–5392.

Purpose: To encourage and reward the qualities of good citizenship.

Area: Citizenship.

Description: The DAR Good Citizens Scholarship Contest consists of two parts. Part I (Personal) is a series of questions asking the student to describe how he or she has tried to manifest the qualities of a Good Citizen. This part may be completed at home and is to be submitted together with a copy of his or her scholastic record and one letter of recommendation. Part II (Essay) is to be administered under the supervision of faculty or DAR member. It must be completed at one sitting, within a two–hour time limit, and without assistance or reference materials. Part I and Part II each represent half of the total contest entry score. Each contest entry is evaluated by independent judges with the first place entry automatically forwarded on to the next level of judging until, ultimately, the final entries are judged on the national level and the national winners are selected.

Eligibility: Males and females may both enter. Program is open to all senior class students enrolled in accredited public or private secondary schools or secondary schools which are in good standing with their state board of education. U.S. citizenship is not a requirement.

Important Dates: DAR national vice chairmen shall have state winner contest entries judged and all first place division winner entries should be sent to national chairman by mid–February.

Competition Origin: 1934.

Guidelines Availability: Information can be obtained through the DAR state chairman in your state.

Deadline: Mid–February.

Winner Notification: Winners are notified by March 10th.

How to Enter: Contact DAR Good Citizen State Chairman of the state in which student resides.

Judging Criteria: Must have qualities of dependability, service, leadership, and patriotism.

Judges: The State Society DAR and the State Department of Education determine the method of selection of the State DAR Good Citizen. School DAR Good Citizen: Each school chooses its own student for this honor.

Awards: The national awards are as follows: First place winner: $5,000 scholarship; second place winner: $2,000; third place winner, $1,000. Each state and division winner receives $250.

Competition: Presidential Classroom.

Sponsor: A Presidential Classroom for Young Americans Inc., 119 Oronoco St., Alexandria, VA 22314.

Purpose: To help prepare outstanding high school juniors and seniors for leadership and civic responsibility by providing firsthand exposure to the federal government in action.

Areas: Leadership and civics.

Description: Each of the one–week sessions in Washington, DC, gives students an "inside" view of government and the American political process. Students meet with and question the country's most influential leaders, discuss issues with peers from across the U.S. and abroad, and visit the historic sites of our nation's capitol. Students renew their self–confidence, gain a broader understanding of government, and continue to build their leadership credentials.

Eligibility: Students must be high school juniors or seniors (rising juniors may attend summer sessions); maintain at least a B average or rank in the top 25 percent of their class; and submit the authorization of their school principal.

Competition Origin: Incorporated in 1968.

Guidelines Availability: Year–round.

Deadline: Registration deadlines of December 1 and May 1 scholarship applications due mid–November.

Winner Notification: Upon receipt and acceptance of application.

How to Enter: Complete application process.

Judging Criteria: See eligibility requirements. Those interested in scholarship opportunities must demonstrate genuine financial need; maintain at least a 3.8 grade point average; and hold leadership positions in school or community organizations.

Judges: Presidential Classroom Staff.

Awards: Limited scholarships available.

Competition: United States Senate Youth Program.

Sponsor: William Randolph Hearst Foundation, 90 New Montgomery St. #1212, San Francisco, CA 94105–4505.

Purpose: To encourage leadership qualities and an interest in government and community service.

Areas: Leadership, service, and government.

Description: The selection process varies by state. The department of education of each state handles the selection process for the foundation.

Eligibility: High school juniors or seniors who are currently serving as elected student body officers. Students must be permanent residents of the state where their parents or legal guardians legally reside.

Competition Origin: 1962.

Guidelines Availability: Information can be requested year–round.

Deadline: Early fall — varies by state.

Winner Notification: Generally, first week of December.

How to Enter: Contact high school principal, state department of education, or call foundation for department of education information.

Judging Criteria: Varies by state.

Awards: 104 $2,000 college scholarships and all–expenses–paid week in Washington, DC.

Advice: Students should start exploring participation in this program soon after the school year begins.

Competition: Washington Crossing Foundation Scholarship Awards.

Sponsor: Washington Crossing Foundation, P.O. Box 17, 1280 General Defermoy Road, Washington Crossing, PA 18977.

Purpose: To provide students in 12th grade who are planning careers in government service an opportunity to express their career plans.

Area: Government careers.

Description: Each interested student is invited to write a one–page essay stating why he or she plans a career in government service including any inspiration to be derived from the leadership of George Washington in his famous crossing of the Delaware.

Eligibility: High school seniors of either gender in the U.S. who are interested in going into government work.

Important Dates: Must be submitted to the foundation by January 15.

Competition Origin: 1969.

Guidelines Availability: Applications are sent to all high schools in United States in September each year.

Deadline: January 15.

Winner Notification: Winners will be notified by telephone by April 15 with confirmation by mail.

How to Enter: Request an application from the Washington Crossing Foundation.

Judging Criteria: The judges' decision will be based on understanding of career requirements, purpose in choice of a career, qualities of leadership exhibited, sincerity, and historical perspective. Semi–finalists may be interviewed by telephone as part of the selection process. All finalists will be interviewed by telephone.

Judges: The board of judges consists of at least three trustees of the Foundation, one member the Washington Crossing Park Commission, and a prominent educator.

Awards: The first–place award of $10,000 is the Ann Hawkes Hutton Scholarship. The second–place award of $7,500 is the I.J. Schekter Scholarship. The third–place award of $5,000 is the Frank and Katharine Davis Scholarship. Each award is paid over a period of four years, if the student meets the requirements of the college chosen, maintains a suitable scholastic level, and continues his or her career objective.

Competition: We the People ... The Citizen and the Constitution, Competitive Congressional Hearings for High School Students.

Sponsor: Center for Civic Education, 5146 Douglas Fir Road, Calabasas, CA 91302.

Purpose: To encourage study and understanding of congressional hearings.

Areas: American history, government, and law–related areas.

Description: Upon completion of the curriculum, teachers involve their entire class in a simulated congressional hearing. A model of performance assessment, the hearing provides an excellent culminating activity and an opportunity for students to demonstrate their knowledge and understanding of the principles of the Constitution and Bill of Rights.

Eligibility: Regularly rostered high school classes in school– scheduled, credit–bearing courses are eligible to participate. Participation in the We the People ... program competitive congressional hearings is limited to high school classes. The program is typically used in conjunction with American government, American history, and/or law–related courses. However, eligibility is not limited to these courses, and it may be used in interdisciplinary programs, language arts courses, or any other course where the subject matter of the program would normally be taught.

Important Dates: August/September — Interested teachers contact the coordinator for the congressional district their school is in and request instructional material. They notify the coordinator of their interest in having their class/classes participate in a competitive congressional hearing.

Fall semester — The teacher teaches the We the People ... program and prepares his or her class/classes to participate in a competitive congressional hearing.
November–January — Vary by state and congressional district– Congressional district level competitive hearings are held.
January–March — Competitive state level congressional hearings are held.
April/May — National level hearings held in Washington, DC.

Competition Origin: The We the People ... program began in the 1986–87 school year under the auspices of the Commission on the Bicentennial of the United States Constitution. The program is funded by an act of the United States Department of Education.

Guidelines Availability: Competition material is available anytime from the congressional district coordinator.

Deadline: End of January.

Winner Notification: District and state level winning classes are announced at the end of the scheduled competitive hearing event. Winning classes are announced at an awards banquet in Washington at the end of a three day nation level hearing.

How to Enter: Have your teacher contact the Center for Civic Education and request the name of the state and district coordinator for the congressional district in which your school is located. He or she should contact the coordinator to request a complimentary set of the We the People ... The Citizen and the Constitution instructional materials and to notify him or her of interest in having the class participate in the competitive hearing at the congressional district level.

Judging Criteria: Each class is divided into six groups, representing the six units of the We the People ... The Citizen and the Constitution textbook. Each group "testifies" before a panel of community representatives taking the role of a congressional committee. The judges score the students' performance on the basis of their knowledge and understanding of the Constitution and Bill or Rights and their ability to apply constitutional principles to historical and contemporary issues. Classes earning the highest scores at the congressional district level go on to a state level hearing. Oral presentations, before another panel of judges, are based on a new set of hearing and follow–up questions. State winners compete each spring in the national finals in Washington, DC. Each judge scores each group (unit) on a scale of 1–10 (10 being the highest) in six categories using a "Congressional Hearing Group Score Sheet." These six categories are: understanding, constitutional application, reasoning, supporting evidence, responsiveness, and participation.

Judges: At the district level, district coordinators select community members and individuals who have professional background and/or experience with the Constitution (lawyers, professors, government officials, etc.). At the state level, judges are selected who have professional experience with the Constitution, and experience serving as judges at the district level. At the national level, judges are nominated by state coordinators. Coordinators are asked to select judges who have professional experience with the Constitution and have preferably judged at the district or state level.

Awards: At the district level, awards for first, second, and third place are distributed. The first place winners from each district progress to state level competition. At the state level, awards for the first, second, and third place are distributed. The first place winners from each state progress to the national level competition. A Certificate of Achievement is awarded to each school. Awards are given for outstanding performance in each of the six unit topics. Awards are given to one class in each of the five geographic regions. Plaques are given to the seven teams placing fourth through tenth. The most important award that classes placing first, second, and third receive is national recognition from adults and peers at the Gala Awards Banquet. Teachers and students also receive medallions.

Advice: Teachers who participate in the competition thoroughly teach the We the People ... curriculum. Competing classes are often coached by lawyers, professors, and other professionals.

Current Events

▼▽▼▽▼▽▼▽▼▽▼▽▼▽▼▽▼▽

Competition: Global Challenge.

Sponsor: National Mathematics League, P.O. Box 9459, Coral Springs, FL 33075.

Purpose: To challenge young minds and encourage an understanding of the people, places, and events that are making our news today and shaping our future tomorrow.

Areas: Current events and geography.

Description: Students in seventh grade through 12th grade may participate. Upon registration the school will receive a letter of confirmation. The school receives the contest for grades 10–12, the contest for grades 7–9 and 100 answer sheets. Additional answer sheets may be purchased if needed. The 45–minute contest consists of 50 multiple-choice questions which encompass topics in national and world news and the geography of these events.

Eligibility: Any middle school, junior high school, or high school may register for Global Challenge.

Important Dates: The contest is administered at the school site on February 1, and the answer sheets are mailed to Global Challenge for electronic scoring.

Guidelines Availability: Each school receives a packet in January.

Deadline: October 31.

Winner Notification: Final results are published in a newsletter which includes pictures and information recognizing the top scoring students and schools.

How to Enter: Contact sponsor or your local school principal or counselor.

Judging Criteria: All answer sheets are machine scored by Global Challenge. Global Challenge tabulates individual and team scores at each grade level. A school receives a team score in each grade level. The team score is the sum of the 10 highest individual scores in a particular grade level.

Awards: Each school will receive ribbons for its top two scoring students in each grade level. All participating students are eligible for national awards, rosette ribbons, which are awarded to the top students in each grade level. Nationally, the schools with the highest team scores receive engraved plaques.

△▲△▲△▲△▲△▲△▲△▲△▲△▲△

Competition: National Current Events League.

Sponsor: National Current Events League, Box 2196, St. James, NY 11780.

Purpose: To improve knowledge of current events.

Area: Current events.

Description: The 35–question meets are held four times a year.

Eligibility: Open to all students in grades 2–12.

Competition Origin: 1993.

Guidelines Availability: Contact sponsor in March.

Deadline: November 1.

Winner Notification: April–May .

How to Enter: Register by mail to sponsor.

Awards: Medals and certificates to winners.

Economics

Competitions: AT&T Collegiate Investment Challenge.

Sponsor: Replica Corporation, Two Technology Way, Norwood, MA 02062.

Purpose: To give students a hands–on stock market experience without risking real money.

Area: Stock market.

Description: Students are given $500,000 in fictitious cash to invest in the stock market over a 10–week period.

Eligibility: Open to students in grades 7–12.

Important Dates: The competition begins in early October. The final date for registration is October 31.

Competition Origin: Began in 1987.

Guidelines Availability: Contact sponsor for a brochure and registration form.

Deadline: The deadline for late registration is October 31.

Winner Notification: A bi–weekly newsletter is sent with a listing of top students.

How to Enter: Contact sponsor.

Judging Criteria: Success of your investment.

Awards: The top 250 students receive an official challenge T–shirt. First–fifth place winners receive lap top computers and scholarships ranging from $500–$2,000. Sixth–50th place winners also receive cash prizes.

Advice: Game packages including a curricular guide and registration are $49.95 per account.

Competition: Economics in One Easy Lesson Essay Contest.

Sponsor: Free Enterprise Institute, 9525 Kate Freeway, Suite 303, Houston, TX 77024–1415.

Purpose: To promote understanding of economic concepts and their application to current events, public policy issues, history, and other subjects.

Area: Economics.

Description: Students write essays that answer topical questions relating to economics.

Eligibility: Open to all high school students.

Important Dates: Guidelines are available in December.

Competition Origin: 1994.

Guidelines Availability: Obtain from sponsor in December.

Deadline: March 31.

Winner Notification: April 15.

How to Enter: Contact sponsor for contest rules, a study guide, and copies of *Economics in One Easy Lesson*.

Judging Criteria: Well–reasoned, well–written essays that answer the topical questions provided in the contest study guide.

Judges: Selected from the Free Enterprise Institute's academic advisors and staff.

Awards: $3,000 — first place; $1,000 — second place; and five third place $500 awards are given. The teacher who encourages each winning student will also be awarded prize money: $300 to the teacher named by the first place winner; $200 second place; and $100 each for third place winners.

General Social Studies

Competition: National History Day Contest.

Sponsor: National History Day Inc., University of Maryland, College Park, MD 20742.

Purpose: To develop critical thinking and problem–solving skills that will help students manage and use information effectively now and in the future. To encourage students to develop a sense of history as process and change, a multi–faceted development over time that affects every aspect of human life and society.

Area: Social studies.

Description: National History Day is a year–long educational program that fosters academic achievement and intellectual growth in secondary school students. By participating in a series of district, state, and national competitions, students develop research and reading skills, refine presentation and performance skills, and develop critical thinking and problem–solving skills that will help them manage and use information effectively now and in the future.

Eligibility: Junior Division includes all students in grades 6, 7, and 8. Senior Division includes all students in grades 9, 10, 11, and 12.

Important Dates: Contact sponsor in late summer or early fall for details.

Competition Origin: 1974 in Cleveland, OH.

Guidelines Availability: Early September.

Winner Notification: Recognized at contest.

How to Enter: Contact sponsor.

Judging Criteria: Varies with area of competition.

Judges: Professionals such as educators and historians.

Awards: At each level of competition, outstanding achievement may be recognized through certificates, medals, trophies, monetary awards, or special prizes that may vary from year to year.

Advice: Successful History Day entries include not only a description of the topic but analysis and interpretation. It is important to place your topic into historical context and perspective. Ask yourself the following questions about your topic: Why is my topic important? How was my topic significant in history in relation to the History Day theme? How did my topic develop over time? How did my topic influence history? How did the events and atmosphere (social, economic, political, and cultural aspects) of my topic's time period influence my topic in history?

Competition: National Social Studies Olympiad.

Sponsor: National Social Studies Olympiad, Box 2196, St. James, NY 11780.

Purpose: To improve social studies skills.

Area: Social studies.

Description: A 50–question test on social studies is administered to participating students.

Eligibility: Open to all students in grades 2–12.

Important Dates: Register by February 10. April 10 is deadline for submission.

Competition Origin: 1993.

Guidelines Availability: Available from sponsor in May.

Winner Notification: May.

How to Enter: Register by mail directed to the sponsor.

Awards: Medals and certificates to winners.

People can succeed at almost anything for which they have unlimited enthusiasm.
—Charles Schwab

Competition: RespecTeen Letter–Writing Contest.

Sponsor: Speak for Yourself Lutheran Brotherhood, 625 Fourth Ave. S, Minneapolis, MN 55415.

Purpose: To encourage students to identify, reflect upon, and act upon issues affecting their lives; to foster communication about youth issues within students' families; and to help students understand how government introduces and passes laws and makes policy decisions.

Areas: Social studies, government, and history.

Description: Students participate in an activity in which letters are written to U.S. representatives about a youth issue, suggesting an approach or solution. One student from each state is invited to a Youth Forum in Washington, DC.

Eligibility: Open to all students in grades 7 and 8.

Competition Origin: 1989.

Guidelines Availability: Write to the sponsor for guidelines. A videotape is also available for preview.

Deadline: January 31 postmark.

How to Enter: Each student must write a letter to the U.S. representative from his or her district discussing an issue affecting young people on a national level and suggesting a solution. The body of the letter should be between 150 and 300 words in length and a standard format must be followed.

Judging Criteria: Issues must be based upon fact. Entries are judged based upon quality and clarity of thought, argument, supporting data, and expression, as well as sincerity and originality. All entries must be in English and those that are not legible will be disqualified.

Judges: Appointed by RespecTeen.

Awards: At the congressional district level, each winner receives a certificate, $50 U.S. Savings Bond, and pending the consent of the representative, personal congratulations from his or her U.S. Representative. At the state level, each winner receives a trip to Washington, DC, including airline tickets, food, and lodging. Each student winner and one parent/guardian participates in the RespecTeen National Youth Forum held in April.

Geography

▼ ▼ ▼ ▼ ▼ ▼ ▼ ▼ ▼ ▼ ▼ ▼ ▼

Competition: Global Challenge.

Sponsor: National Mathematics League, P.O. Box 9459, Coral Springs, FL 33075.

Purpose: To challenge young minds and encourage an understanding of the people, places, and events that are making our news today and shaping our future tomorrow.

Areas: Current events and geography.

Description: Students in seventh grade through 12th grade may participate. Upon registration the school will receive a letter of confirmation. The school receives the contest for grades 10–12, the contest for grades 7–9, and 100 answer sheets. Additional answer sheets may be purchased if needed. The 45–minute contest consists of 50 multiple-choice questions which encompass topics in national and world news and the geography of these events.

Eligibility: Any middle school, junior high school, or high school may register for Global Challenge.

Important Dates: The contest is administered at the school site on February 1, and the answer sheets are mailed to Global Challenge for electronic scoring.

Guidelines Availability: Each school receives a packet in January.

Deadline: October 31.

Winner Notification: Final results are published in a newsletter which includes pictures and information recognizing the top scoring students and schools.

How to Enter: Contact sponsor or your local school principal or counselor.

Judging Criteria: All answer sheets are machine scored by Global Challenge. Global Challenge tabulates individual and team scores at each grade level. A school receives a team score in each grade level. The team score is the sum of the 10 highest individual scores in a particular grade level.

Awards: Each school will receive ribbons for its top two scoring students in each grade level. All participating students are eligible for national awards, rosette ribbons, which are awarded to the top students in each grade level. Nationally, the schools with the highest team scores receive engraved plaques.

▲ ▲ ▲ ▲ ▲ ▲ ▲ ▲ ▲ ▲ ▲ ▲ ▲

Competition: Junior Scholastic Find the Map Man.

Sponsor: Junior Scholastic, 555 Broadway, New York, NY 10012.

Purpose: To encourage students to use the map–reading and geography skills that they have learned in the magazine in competing for prizes and national recognition.

Areas: Map knowledge and map drawing.

Description: Students must find the Map Man by reading two maps and correctly answering questions based on the maps. The correct answers lead students to the mystery location, of which they must then draw a map.

Eligibility: Open to all Junior Scholastic readers. The magazine is published for grades 6–8, but it is read by some younger and some older students.

Important Dates: Contest appears in two consecutive November issues. Entries must be postmarked by December 1, and winners are announced in the February issue.

Guidelines Availability: See November issues of Junior Scholastic.

Deadline: Postmarked by December 1.

Winner Notification: Winners announced in February issue of Junior Scholastic.

How to Enter: Follow directions for entry as described in November issues of Junior Scholastic.

Judging Criteria: Entries are judged based upon originality, accuracy, attention to detail, artistic merit, creativity, originality, and execution.

Judges: The person who draws all of the maps appearing in the magazine is the judge.

Awards: The entry with the most correct answers and the best, most original map will win the grand prize of a $500 U.S. Savings Bond. Runners-up receive Map Man T–shirts. Special awards are given to school classrooms that submit the best entries.

Competition: National Geography Bee.

Sponsor: National Geographic Society, 1145 17th St. N.W., Washington, DC 20036–4688.

Purpose: To encourage the teaching and study of geography.

Area: Geography.

Description: Principals of schools must register and each school conducts the first competition, consisting of both oral and written elements. The student winners progress through the qualifying test, state, and national level competitions.

Eligibility: Any student in grades 4–8.

Important Dates: School level competitions are held early December through mid–January. State level competitions held in early spring. National level competitions are held in late May.

Guidelines Availability: Write to National Geographic Society for details.

Deadline: Registration deadline is mid–October for schools who wish to hold a bee.

Winner Notification: Winners are named on the date of competition.

How to Enter: Principals must register their schools before the October deadline to participate in the program.

Judging Criteria: Based on correctness and completeness of answers to oral and written questions concerning geography.

Judges: At the school and qualifying test level a school representative is the judge. A state bee coordinator administrates at the state level, and The National Geographic Society administrates the national competition.

Awards: Prizes vary according to the level of competition. The national level awards first place a $25,000 college scholarship; second place receives a $15,000 college scholarship; third place receives a $10,000 college scholarship. The top 10 finalists receive $500 each and prizes are given to the schools of the top 10 winners.

Competition: National Geography Olympiad.

Sponsor: National Geography Olympiad, Box 2196, St. James, NY 11780.

Purpose: To improve geography skills.

Area: Geography.

Description: The 50–question test is administered in late April, early May.

Eligibility: Open to all students in grades 2–12.

Important Dates: Register by February 10. April 10 is deadline for test to be taken.

Competition Origin: 1986.

Guidelines Availability: Request from sponsor in May.

Winner Notification: Announced in May.

How to Enter: Register by mail to the sponsor.

Awards: Medals and certificates are given to the winners.

If you think you can, you can. And if you think you can't, you're right.
—Mary Kay Ash

Global Issues

Competition: UNA–USA National High School Essay Contest on the United Nations.

Sponsor: United Nations Association of the United States of America, 485 Fifth Ave., New York, NY 10017.

Purpose: To engage students in grades 9–12 nationwide in a serious research and writing exercise about the United Nations and the issues confronting the world organization and to broaden the perspectives of American students to better understand the complexities of our world and the challenges our nation faces as a member of the international community.

Area: Global issues.

Description: High school students write and submit essays on the United Nations.

Eligibility: Open to all students in grades 9–12.

Important Dates: The topic for the contest is announced and distributed to participating chapters, divisions, and affiliated organizations of UNA–USA in September. UNA–USA staff produces promotional materials and information about the contest that is distributed to participating groups in the contest. Participating chapters, divisions, and affiliated organizations of UNA–USA organize and conduct local contests for high school students in their area. Deadline for students submitting essays to participating chapters, divisions, and affiliated organizations is March 1. The national competition among the top essays submitted from each local contest is conducted in April. The finalists are judged in the latter part of April. The three national prize–winning essays are announced in May.

Competition Origin: 1985.

Guidelines Availability: Obtain from sponsor in September.

Deadline: March 1.

Winner Notification: May.

How to Enter: To enter the program, teachers and students are encouraged to contact their local United Nations Association chapter or the sponsor.

Judging Criteria: Decisions based upon research and writing, as well as

demonstration of an understanding of the issue.

Judges: National panel of experts.

Awards: Three awards are given annually: cash awards of $1,000 (first prize); $750 (second prize); and $500 (third prize) and an all–expenses–paid trip for the prize–winning students and their teachers to New York City for the awards ceremony.

Competition: United Nations Pilgrimage for Youth.

Sponsor: The Odd Fellows and Rebekahs, P.O. Box 1778, Palm Harbor, FL 34682–1778.

Purpose: To study and learn about the United Nations.

Area: Global issues.

Description: Students complete a U.N. exam, submit an essay, and/or participate in a speech contest. Selected winners receive an expense–paid trip to New York City.

Eligibility: Open to students ages 16–17.

Important Dates: Dates vary. Make application for more information.

Competition Origin: June 1950.

Guidelines Availability: Contact local Odd Fellow and/or Rebekah Lodges.

Winner Notification: Prior to June trip.

How to Enter: Contact local Odd Fellow and/or Rebekah Lodges.

Judging Criteria: Applications are reviewed by selecting committees for evidence of scholarship, leadership, character, extra–curricular activities, concern for community welfare, interest in world affairs, and general fitness to participate in the program.

Awards: Each year, during June and July, North American students travel by bus to and from New York City, visiting monuments and places of interest on the way. The Odd Fellows and Rebekahs sponsor the entire cost of the tour. They are housed four to a room in New York, sharing with students from as far away as Australia, Denmark, Finland, Germany, Norway, Sweden, and Switzerland. The week–long schedule includes four half day visits to the United Nations where students are allowed to listen to behind–the–scenes briefings on specialized U.N. agencies and departments, witness a council or committee in action, see business conducted in the six official languages of the U.N., and take a guided tour.

Advice: Students who are interested should contact their local Odd Fellow and/or Rebekah Lodges.

Technology

Competition: American Computer Science League Competitions.

Sponsor: American Computer Science League, Association of Computer Science Leagues Inc., Box 40118, Providence, RI 02940.

Purpose: To provide a unique and exciting educational opportunity for computer enthusiasts. Contest problems motivate students to study computer topics not covered in their school's curricula and to pursue classroom topics in depth.

Area: Computers.

Description: Contests are held at each participating school thereby eliminating the need for travel, and an unlimited number of students from all grade levels may compete at each school. A school's score is the sum of the scores of its three or five highest–scoring students. In each competition, students are given short theoretical and applied questions, and then a practical problem to solve within the following three days, testing it on our data using their school's computer facilities. After the contest is administered by the faculty advisor, each school's results are returned to ACSL for tabulation. At the end of the year, an Invitational Team All–Star Contest is held at a common site. The Classroom Division consists of only pencil and paper questions; there are no programming problems. This division is open to all students from all grades not competing in any other division. Prizes are awarded on a grade–by–grade basis.

Eligibility: Junior and senior high school students. The Senior Division is geared to those high school students with experience programming computers, especially those taking a computer science AP course. It is suggested that schools do not register for the Senior Division during their first year of ACSL participation.

The Intermediate Division is geared to senior high school students with little or no computer programming experience and to advanced junior high students. The Junior Division is designed for junior high and middle school students with no previous experience programming computers.

The Classroom Division is open to students from all grades. It consists of a selection of the non–programming problems from the other three divisions. As its name implies, this division is particularly well–suited for use in the classroom.

Competition Origin: 1979.

Guidelines Availability: Contact sponsor.

Deadline: Dates vary with each competition.

Awards: The grand prizes are 12 copies of Microsoft Visual Basic, Visual C++, and Microsoft Office Programs. These are awarded to the top school in each division at the Team All–Star Contest. Also at the All–Star Contest, trophies are awarded to top teams in each division and to each team member of those schools. Books are awarded to top scoring students by grade. During the regular season, trophies are awarded to the top teams and top individuals in each regional area of each division. Each team receives an award to present to an outstanding student at the advisor's discretion.

Competitions: Global SchoolNet Foundation.

Sponsor: Global SchoolNet Foundation, 7040 Avenida Encinas, Suite 104–281, Carlsbad, CA 92009.

Areas: All academic areas are covered.

Description: Students go to Global SchoolNet's World Wide Web site where they will find five to 10 questions having to do with the academics that are presented there. If they answer the questions correctly, their names are placed in a drawing where they are eligible for prizes.

Eligibility: Any elementary or secondary students from around the USA and the world are eligible.

Competition Origin: October 1, 1995.

Guidelines Availability: From the World Wide Web address or by writing to the sponsor.

Deadline: This is an on–going, year–round contest. Each contest starts the first of every month and ends the last day of each month.

Winner Notification: Notification through E–mail, U.S. mail, or by phone on the last day of each month.

How to Enter: School or student must be connected to the Internet and have access to the World Wide Web. The contestant goes to the following address: http://gsn.org. All the simple rules are listed there. Contestants may enter as often as they like.

Judging Criteria: Students must get all of the questions correct. All answers to the questions are found at the same World Wide Web site, some "digging" and exploring will have to be done to find the correct answers. Five prizes are given away each month. If there are more than five students with the correct answers in any given month, then those names will be randomly drawn to determine the five winners for that month.

Awards: Prizes include: miscellaneous software including educational, word processing, graphics, and games; computer books; computer accessories, including modems; denim jackets; t–shirts; ball caps; pizza parties; and movie tickets. The value of individual prizes range from $20 to $600.

Competition: International Student Media Festival.

Sponsor: The Association for Educational Communications and Technology International Student Media Festival, AACUPS–2644 Riva Road, Annapolis, MD 21401.

Purpose: To encourage student media production.

Areas: Animation, computer-generated, multimedia, live action, and sequential still images.

Description: More than 200 student entries of seven minutes or less are entered from students representing many states.

Eligibility: Students kindergarten through college.

Important Dates: October 1 is the competition deadline.

Competition Origin: 1980.

Guidelines Availability: Contact the sponsor in April.

Deadline: October 1.

Winner Notification: November.

How to Enter: Write to the sponsor and ask to be placed on the entry form mailing list.

Judging Criteria: Creativity, originality, organization/purpose, continuity/structure, relevance/importance, documentation, use of available resources, clarity, and energy/education.

Awards: Students receive certificates and critiques. Winners can also attend an awards ceremony.

Competition: Toshiba NSTA ExploraVision Awards Program.

Sponsor: National Science Teachers Association, 1840 Wilson Blvd., Arlington, VA 22201.

Purpose: To provide opportunities for K–12 students to enhance or design technologies that could exist in the future.

Area: Futuristic technology design.

Description: This is the world's largest science contest in which teams of three to four students in grades K–12 expand on or design technologies that could exist 20 years in the future.

Eligibility: Open to all students in grades K–12.

Important Dates: February 1 is the entry deadline; in mid–March the 48 regional semi–finalist teams are announced; in mid– April videos are due from the semi–finalists; in the beginning of May the 12 finalist teams are announced and in early June the four first–place winners (one from each grade category) and the eight second–place teams (two from each grade category) are announced at a press conference that is the kick–off to an awards weekend.

Competition Origin: 1992.

Guidelines Availability: Contact the sponsor in September.

Deadline: February 1.

Winner Notification: Winners are notified in early June.

How to Enter: Students participate in teams of three or four with a teacher–adviser and an optional community advisor in one of four grade levels K–3, 4–6, 7–9, and 10–12, must be under 21 years of age, and be a full–time student in an accredited institution. By February 1 the teams must submit a teacher–signed entry form, a 10–page or fewer typed description of their technology, and story boards depicting scenes from a sample five–minute video they would produce to convey their ideas.

Judging Criteria: Decisions are based upon creativity, scientific accuracy, communication, and feasibility of vision.

Judges: Leading science educators serve as judges.

Awards: The 48 regional semi–finalist teams each receive $500 to produce the video for the final judging. Each student who enters and each teacher and community advisor who sponsors a team will receive a certificate of participation and a small gift. The schools of the 48 semi–finalist teams will receive a television and a VCR. The 36 semi–finalist team members who do not go on to the finals each receive a $100 savings bond. Schools of the 12 finalist teams each receive a Toshiba product such as a FAX machine, copier, etc. The teacher advisors of the 12 finalists' teams also receive a Toshiba product. The 12 finalist team members, their teachers, and parents will be given a trip to Washington, DC, in June for the awards ceremony. Student members of the four first–place teams each receive a $10,000 savings bond while the students on the eight second–place teams each receive a $5,000 savings bond.

Competition: USA Computing Olympiad.

Sponsor: University of Wisconsin–Parkside, 900 Wood Road, Kenosha, WI 53141–2000.

Purpose: To select the team of four students to represent the United States in the annual International Olympiad in Informatics (IOI).

Areas: Problem solving and computer programming.

Description: The goals of the USACO are to: provide U.S. students with opportunities to sharpen their computing skills enabling them to compete successfully at the international level, enhance the quality of computer education in U.S. high schools by providing students and teachers with challenging programming problems which emphasize algorithm development and problem solving skills, and select the U.S. team to attend the annual International Olympiad in Informatics.

To achieve these goals, the USACO conducts the following activities:

> **Qualifying Round.** A general qualifying round is held in February where all interested students in the United States are challenged to solve at least two problems from a set of five within a period of one week. Those who are successful advance to the Challenge Round.

> **Challenge Round.** A closely monitored round held in March when all qualified students in the United States are challenged to solve three problems in five hours. The problems are administered to students in their local area and ranked by the USACO judges.

> **Final Round.** The 16 top ranked students from the Challenge Round are invited to a week–long training and selection program held in the summer at the University of Wisconsin–Parkside. At the conclusion of the week, the top four students are selected to become the United States team at the annual International Olympiad in Informatics.

> **IOI Competition.** The U.S. team travels to the annual IOI Competition later in the summer.

Eligibility: Participants must be high school students in the United States.

Competition Origin: The USA Computing Olympiad is similar in philosophy and operating structure to the USA Mathematics Olympiad (established in 1972), the USA Physics Olympiad (established in 1986), and the USA Chemistry Olympiad (established in 1974). It was established at the University of Wisconsin–Parkside in 1992.

Guidelines Availability: Information about the USACO and IOI is available from the sponsor.

Deadline: January 15.

Winner Notification: The USA team is notified at the end of the final round held at the University of Wisconsin–Parkside.

How to Enter: Contact a high school or college teacher who will serve as a local coordinator. Have the local coordinator contact the USACO at the location shown above.

Judging Criteria: The winners are selected based on their performance at the final round of the USACO.

Judges: The staff of the USACO serve as judges.

Awards: The 13–16 finalists in the Competition Round receive a week long, all–expenses–paid trip to the Final Round at the University of Wisconsin–Parkside. The USACO team receives an all–expenses–paid trip to the International Olympiad in Informatics which is held in a different country each year and lasts for 10 days.

FINE AND PERFORMING ARTS COMPETITIONS

Drawing and Poster Design

Competition: AAA National Traffic Safety Poster Program.

Sponsor: American Automobile Association, 1000 AAA Dr., Heathrow, FL 32746–5063.

Purpose: To teach and promote traffic safety.

Areas: Traffic safety and visual arts.

Description: Create and execute a chosen traffic safety slogan in the form of a poster. Guidelines: poster size — either 15" x 20", 14" x 22", or 12" x 18" leaving a 3" margin across the bottom of the poster for entry blank and administrative purposes.

Eligibility: Kindergarten through 12th grade including all nationally recognized girls and boys clubs.

Competition Origin: National Traffic Safety Department of the American Automobile Association.

Guidelines Availability: Available from the local main AAA club office.

Deadline: Early February.

Winner Notification: Will be made from local AAA Clubs.

How to Enter: Mail finished poster to either the main local office of AAA or to AAA National Headquarters as noted in the Poster Program brochure guidelines.

Judging Criteria: Relationship of the poster design to traffic safety practices, originality of the poster, artwork, and execution.

Judges: A panel of prominent individuals in the fields of education, art, and traffic safety.

Awards: U.S. Saving Bonds are awarded to the winners, amounts ranging from $75 to $500.

Advice: Have a focal point, keep it simple. Use contrasting colors. Viewers must be able to read quickly and not analyze.

Competition: Federal Junior Duck Stamp Conservation and Design Program.

Sponsor: U.S. Fish and Wildlife Service, Federal Duck Stamp Office, 1849 C St. N.W., Washington, DC 20240.

Purpose: To teach wetlands awareness and conservation through the arts to students kindergarten through high school.

Areas: Designs of North American ducks, swans, or geese in natural habitats.

Description: The JDS program is a curriculum–based art education program for kindergarten through high school students. One of the activities suggested in the curriculum guide is designing a Junior Duck Stamp — a stamp that is sold by the Wildlife service every year — and entering that design in the state JDS contest.

Eligibility: Open to all K–12 students.

Important Dates: Contact the state sponsor.

Competition Origin: 1989.

Guidelines Availability: Information is mailed to schools in October. Teachers may write to sponsor for a free curriculum guide and a JDS video.

Deadline: Varies with each state competition.

Winner Notification: November.

How to Enter: Mail your design to your state sponsor.

Judging Criteria: Accurate depiction of wildlife in its natural habitat.

Judges: Each state selects five judges.

Awards: The U.S. Fish and Wildlife Service awards a certificate of participation to each student who enters a design, 100 ribbons across all age categories, and a State Best of Show ribbon. In some states, sponsors may offer additional prizes. The national first, second, and third place winners, their art teachers, and one of their parents win a free trip to Washington, DC, to attend the Federal Duck Stamp Contest. The first place winner also receives a $2,500 award.

▼ ▾ ▼ ▾ ▼ ▾ ▼ ▾ ▼ ▾ ▼ ▾ ▼

Competition: The Lions International Peace Poster.

Sponsor: Lions Clubs International, 300 22nd St., Oak Brook, IL, 60521–8842.

Purpose: To give young people the opportunity to express their thoughts about world peace in an original artwork.

Area: Posters.

Description: Posters are judged at the school level and there are two more rounds to reach international competition and the grand prize. Themes change from year to year.

Eligibility: Open to all children, male and female, ages 11–13.

Important Dates: Sponsorship requests should be entered by October 1st. School competitions must be completed by November 30th.

Competition Origin: 1988.

Guidelines Availability: Teachers and principals must contact the Lions Clubs International.

Winner Notification: Winners are notified at each level of competition as it occurs. International winners are notified no later than March 1.

How to Enter: School teachers or principals should contact Lions Clubs International.

Judging Criteria: Posters are judged according to originality, artistic merit, and expression of theme.

Judges: Throughout the judging process, posters are evaluated by different groups of judges. On the international level, they are judged by internationally renowned people involved with art, peace, or children.

Advice: No one may enter the contest independently. Students and schools must be sponsored by a local Lions Club to participate.

▲ ▲ ▲ ▲ ▲ ▲ ▲ ▲ ▲ ▲ ▲ ▲ ▲

Competition: Mothers Against Drunk Driving Annual Poster/Essay Contest.

Sponsor: Mothers Against Drunk Driving, 5111 E. John Carpenter Frwy., Suite 700, Irving, TX 75062–8187.

Purpose: To provide an excellent opportunity for students to express their creativity and educate their families and peers about the dangers of underage drinking.

Areas: Essay writing and poster design.

Description: This is an annual competition designed to reach current and future drivers many of whom are directly affected by alcohol–related crashes. Students may choose to enter a poster or an essay.

Eligibility: Open to students in grades 1–12.

Guidelines Availability: The rules, entry form, and the annual theme are available in the early fall each year.

Deadline: Each year the MADD National Office sets and announces a national entry deadline. All entries from first place winners in local or statewide contests and from those entering the "Individual Competition" must be postmarked by the national entry date and mailed to the MADD National Office.

Winner Notification: The national winners are notified by telephone and letter within one week of judging.

How to Enter: Obtain entry form from local MADD chapters or by contacting the MADD National Office.

Judging Criteria: Originality, uniqueness, reflection of creative thinking, style, expression, attractiveness, use of color, artistic ability, degree of visual impact, and appropriateness and relationship to contest theme.

Judges: Judges are chosen who have qualifications in education, art, writing, design, substance abuse prevention, traffic safety, etc.

Awards: Prizes vary from year to year.

Competition: National Americanism Poster Contest.

Sponsor: AMVETS National Headquarters, 4647 Forbes Blvd., Lanham, MD 20706–4380.

Purpose: To promote Americanism among youth.

Area: Drawing.

Description: All students must address the theme. Themes change annually. Entries must be free–hand drawings using pen, pencil, crayon, paint, or any combination of these media. Gluing pictures or other materials to the surface of the drawing is not allowed. The student's description of the drawing must be written on the back of the poster in 50 words or fewer. Entry descriptions that are stapled, taped, or otherwise attached will not be accepted. Entries must not be larger than 11½" by 15" using construction paper or poster board.

Eligibility: All students in the third and fifth grades who are attending public, private, or parochial schools.

Important Dates: National entries must be postmarked by July 1.

Guidelines Availability: Contact sponsor.

Deadline: All national entries must be postmarked by July 1. Local and state deadlines may vary.

How to Enter: Contact local sponsor for dates and times.

Awards: First prize — $150 savings bond and plaque; second prize — $100 savings bond; and third prize — $50 savings bond.

Competition: National Women's Hall of Fame Poster and Essay Contest.

Sponsor: National Women's Hall of Fame, P.O. Box 335, 76 Fall St., Seneca Falls, NY 13148.

Purpose: To provide youth an opportunity to express their ideas and feelings through visual arts.

Areas: Poster and essay.

Description: Entries must be no smaller than 16" x 20" and no larger than 22" x 28". Entries must be on mat board or illustration board. Mailings should be packaged and sent flat, not in a mailing tube. Each poster must limit collage–type art to 20 percent of the poster, the remaining being original, illustrative work. Attach a copy of the official entry form securely to each poster entered. All entries become the property of NWHF, and no entries can be returned.

Eligibility: The contest is open to all students enrolled in grades 7 through 12.

Guidelines Availability: Ongoing.

Deadline: March 31.

Winner Notification: May.

How to Enter: Write for guidelines.

Judging Criteria: The posters will be judged on a combination of factors including: adherence to theme, creativity, originality, and artistic merit.

Awards: The top three entrants in each essay level and poster category receive a Certificate of Achievement and cash prizes. The first prize winner receives $100; the second prize winner receives $75; and the third prize winner receives $50.

Competition: U.S. Savings Bonds National Student Poster Contest.

Sponsor: Sponsor pending but inquiries should be addressed to: Coordinator, National Student Poster Contest, Savings Bonds Marketing Office, Department of the Treasury, Bureau of the Public Debt, Washington, DC 20226.

Purpose: To promote creativity and to encourage children to think about savings and promote good savings habits at a young age.

Area: Art.

Description: Students are to create a poster for U.S. Savings Bonds.

Eligibility: Open to students in 4–6 grades.

Competition Origin: Contest began in 1991.

Guidelines Availability: Poster contest kits are available in September.

Deadline: Winter.

Winner Notification: Spring.

How to Enter: Participants need to get an entry form from their school to enter.

Judging Criteria: Creativity, originality, conveys theme, and artistic ability.

Judges: A judging chair selects judges.

Awards: State Prizes: first place winner — $1,000 U.S. Savings Bond, second place winner — $500 U.S. Savings Bond, and third place winner — $200 U.S. Savings Bond; National prizes: first place winner — $5,000 U.S. Savings Bond, second place winner — $1,000 U.S. Savings Bond, and third place winner — $500 U.S. Savings Bond.

Music

Competition: Delius Composition Contest for High School Composers.

Sponsor: The Delius Association, College of Fine Arts, Jacksonville, FL 32211.

Purpose: To recognize original compositions across a variety of musical media.

Areas: Vocal, keyboard, and instrumental.

Description: High school students submit original scores for national competition.

Eligibility: Grades 10–12.

Important Dates: Submit scores by October.

Competition Origin: 1985.

Guidelines Availability: Contact sponsor.

Deadline: October 1.

Winner Notification: Announced at Annual Delius Festival in Jacksonville, FL.

How to Enter: Entry fee of $5 must accompany application. Contact sponsor for details for submission.

Judges: Secret panel of judges designated by Delius Association of Florida.

Awards: $200 first prize and $100 second prize.

Competition: MTNA – CCP/Belwin Student Composition Competition.

Sponsor: Music Teachers National Association, The Carew Tower, 441 Vine St., Suite 505, Cincinnati, OH 45202–2814.

Purpose: To encourage creativity and self–expression in student musicians through composing and to recognize their achievements and their teachers.

Area: Music composition.

Description: Students from each state submit one composition in the form of manuscripts either computer–generated or handwritten. The piece can be for any medium but may not last longer than 10 minutes. The compositions are judged at the state level with the winners in each category being sent to one of seven regional divisions. The four winners in each of these divisions are then sent to the national coordinator who in turn sends them to three national judges. Four winners and first and second runners–up are declared. The four national winners have their compositions performed at the MTNA National Convention held usually in March.

Eligibility: Elementary — up to fifth grade; junior — up to ninth grade; senior high — grades 9 through 12; and collegiate.

Important Dates: All compositions are due at the state level by September 1. All compositions are due at the division level by November 1. All compositions are due at the national level by December 15.

Guidelines Availability: June/July issue of *American Music Teacher Magazine*.

Winner Notification: January 15.

How to Enter: A student's composition teacher must be a member of MTNA; all rules, regulations, and forms are available to all MTNA teachers.

Judging Criteria: Compositions are judged according to rhythm (metric invention); harmony (vertical language); melody (horizontal materials); timbre (tone color, dynamic control, orchestral skills); stylistic consistency; and notation.

Judges: State, division, and national judges are selected by the respective state, division, and national composition chairs.

Awards: Financial awards vary from state to state and from division to division. National awards are $300 for elementary; $400 for junior high; $700 for senior high; and $1,000 for collegiate.

Competition: National Federation of Music Clubs Scholarships and Awards.

Sponsor: National Federation of Music Clubs, 1336 North Delaware St., Indianapolis, IN 46202.

Purpose: To develop and enhance student skills in music.

Areas: Instrumental, composition, voice, and theory.

Description: Scholarships and awards in music are granted through a variety of student competitions.

Eligibility: Junior age — must not have reached the 19th birthday by March; student age — must have reached 16th but not 26th birthday by March 1. Entrants of 16, 17, and 18 years may enter either junior or student competitions but not both at the same time.

Important Dates: Vary with competitions.

Guidelines Availability: Upon receipt of scholarship and awards chart from sponsor, write directly to each specific scholarship of interest.

Winner Notification: Varies with competition.

How to Enter: Write to sponsor for scholarship and awards chart.

Judging Criteria: Exemplifies excellence in area of competition.

Judges: Music professionals.

Awards: Cash scholarships ranging from $10 to $10,000, private lesson fees to full tuition.

Competition: Panasonic Young Soloists Award.

Sponsor: Very Special Arts, Education Office, The John F. Kennedy Center for Performing Arts, Washington, DC 20566.

Purpose: To recognize exceptional young musicians with disabilities.

Areas: Instrumental and vocal.

Description: Applicants are required to complete an application form and submit a brief autobiography as well as a videotape or audio cassette recording.

Eligibility: Award is given to musically talented students, ages 25 and under, with a disability.

Guidelines Availability: Contact sponsor.

Deadline: September 10.

Winner Notification: January.

How to Enter: Request application packet from sponsor.

Judges: Professional musicians and music educators.

Awards: Soloists who earn scholarship funds are invited to perform at The John F. Kennedy Center for the Performing Arts.

▼ ▼ ▼ ▼ ▼ ▼ ▼ ▼ ▼ ▼ ▼ ▼ ▼ ▼ ▼

Competition: Reflections Cultural Arts Program.

Sponsor: The National PTA, 330 N. Wabash Ave., Suite 2100, Chicago, IL 60611.

Purpose: To provide opportunities for students in pre–school through the 12th grade to express and share their creative abilities.

Areas: Literature, music, photography, and visual arts.

Description: This competition is designed to give preschool through high school age students opportunities to express and share their creation. Each year works of art are inspired by a theme which is chosen from hundreds of student theme entries.

Eligibility: Any PTA/PTSA in good standing may sponsor the Reflections Program. Students must participate in Reflections through their local PTA/PTSA. The National PTA does not limit the number of entries a student may submit. Local and state PTAs may set limitations at their discretion.

Important Dates: Contact state PTA for dates.

Guidelines Availability: Available from state PTA.

Deadline: Varies for each state.

Winner Notification: Each state president receives a list in May. All participants receive a certificate and letter of congratulation or regret at this time.

How to Enter: State PTAs submit entries to national level.

Awards: The National PTA awards first, second, and third place in each arts area in each grade division. Honorable mentions may be chosen in each art category and grade division. Place winners receive a cash prize ($300, $200, or $100), a certificate, and a book is donated to each of their schools. One outstanding interpretation winner is chosen from the place winners in each arts area (a total of four). These winners receive an expense–paid trip to the National PTA convention with one adult, a $250 scholarship, and a gold–plated Reflections medallion.

Advice: Each entry must be the work of one student. Each student and his or her parent or guardian must sign the affirmation sentence on the Official Entry Form stating that the entry is original.

▲ ▲ ▲ ▲ ▲ ▲ ▲ ▲ ▲ ▲ ▲ ▲ ▲ ▲ ▲ ▲

Competition: Reflections Scholarship Competition.

Sponsor: The National PTA, 330 N. Wabash Ave., Suite 2100, Chicago, IL 60611–3690.

Purpose: To provide scholarships for students wishing to pursue arts in their future education.

Areas: Literature, music, photography, and visual arts.

Description: The Reflections Scholarship Competition consists of four scholarships of $750 each, one in each of four arts areas: literature, music, photography, and visual arts. It is directed toward students who wish to pursue the arts in their future education.

Eligibility: Each student must be a senior in high school.

Important Dates: Deadline for requesting application is the last Friday in November.

Guidelines Availability: Contact sponsor.

Deadline: The deadline for requesting an application is the last Friday in November. After that date applications may be requested from your state PTA office. All requests must include the national ID number for your local PTA unit which can be acquired through your local unit president or state office.

Winner Notification: Announced in March.

How to Enter: Submit two original works. Submit a completed application packet including: a personal essay, completed entry forms (with signed verification from the local PTA president and national ID number for the local PTA unit), and a teacher's letter of recommendation (including recommendation form).

Judging Criteria: Judging criteria include maturity of work, articulation of personal goals in the essay, and teacher's letter of recommendation.

Judges: A jury is assembled from professionals from each arts area.

Awards: Four scholarships of $750 each.

▼ ▾ ▼ ▾ ▼ ▾ ▼ ▾ ▼ ▾ ▼ ▾ ▼ ▾ ▼ ▾

Competition: Scholastic Inc. and Elektra Entertainment's WRITE LYRICS Contest, co–sponsored by Microsoft.

Sponsor: Scholastic Inc., 555 Broadway, New York, NY 10012.

Purpose: To encourage students and teachers to consider songwriting as a legitimate medium for study and self–expression.

Area: Lyric writing.

Description: Participants write an original song lyric and compete for the grand prize of an in–school performance by an Elektra artist.

Eligibility: Open to all students in grades 6–12, except those who have family members employed by Scholastic Inc., Elektra Entertainment, or Microsoft.

Competition Origin: 1993.

Guidelines Availability: Contest information and official entry forms are available in mid–January to teacher subscribers of Scholastic's classroom magazines *Scope, Junior Scholastic, Action, Literary Cavalcade, Choices*, and *Update*. Check with your school librarian.

Deadline: Entries are due in early April.

Winner Notification: Winners are notified by early May.

How to Enter: Send an original song lyric, not necessarily based on a specific tune, and an official entry form or facsimile.

Judging Criteria: Creativity, clarity, and quality of thinking, not on music, length, or presentation.

Judges: Scholastic's classroom magazine editors and representatives of Elektra Entertainment conduct initial judging. Semi–final entries are then sent to a recording artist who makes the final selection of the grand–prize winner and runners–up.

Awards: The grand prize is an in–school performance by an Elektra Entertainment recording artist. Other prizes include recordings by the participating Elektra Entertainment artist, and computers and computer software.

△ ▲ △ ▲ △ ▲ △ ▲ △ ▲ △ ▲ △ ▲ △ ▲ △

Butterflies are good! Convert nervousness into excitement.

—12-year-old girl

Performing Arts

Competition: Donna Reed Foundation for the Performing Arts.

Sponsor: The Donna Reed Foundation for the Performing Arts, Scholarship Division, P.O. Box 122, Denison, IA 51442.

Purpose: To support talented individuals who desire to pursue an education or a career in the performing arts.

Areas: Dance (ballet, modern, jazz, tap); vocal (classical and musical theater); instrumental (classical and musical theater); acting for stage or screen, directing for stage or screen, and writing for stage or screen.

Description: Based on level of talent, applicants submit audio or videotapes of their work or scripts and recommendations from teachers or professionals and a statement from the applicant about his or her plans and future goals in performing arts.

Eligibility: Available to high school seniors qualified to enter an undergraduate college program (program may be expanding to include college level).

Important Dates: Application deadline is March 1. Notification to finalists is April 15. Donna Reed Festival of Workshops is in mid–June.

Competition Origin: 1987.

Guidelines Availability: January.

Deadline: March 1.

Winner Notification: June 9–15.

Judges: Judges are selected from the head or chairmanship of performing arts departments (music, dance, theater, writing, communications, etc.) from major colleges as well as practicing professionals in the various disciplines (symphony conductors, chorus directors, directors of theater companies, etc.).

Awards: One $10,000 four–year scholarship to any four–year undergraduate program the winner chooses; eight full–tuition, all–expenses–paid scholarships to the Donna Reed Festival of Workshops in June; 8–16 full–tuition only scholarships to the Donna Reed Festival of Workshops in June.

Photography and Videotaping

Competition: American Morgan Horse Association for Youth Photo Contest.

Sponsor: AMHAY Photo Contest, American Morgan Horse Association, P.O. Box 960, Shelburne, VT 05482–0960.

Purpose: To provide students an opportunity to demonstrate their creative abilities through photography.

Area: Photography.

Description: Using "Morgan at Play" as a theme, submit a photograph containing a registered Morgan horse and give it a caption. Color or black and white prints 5" x 7" or 8" x 10" in size must be submitted.

Eligibility: Junior photographers — ages 18 and under.

Important Dates: Entries must be postmarked December 1.

Guidelines Availability: Contact sponsor in early fall.

Deadline: December 1.

Winner Notification: Upon completion of judging.

How to Enter: Photographs may be color or black and white prints, 5" x 7" or 8" x 10" in size. Mounting of photos is desirable but not required. A $2 entry fee is required for each photo. Photographers may enter as many photographs as they wish. Entries must be postmarked by December 1. A separate entry form must be used for each photo submitted. The entry form must be attached to the back of the photo.

Judging Criteria: Photos will be judged on creativity, spontaneity of subject, technical quality, breed promotion, and overall appearance.

Judges: American Morgan Horse Association Officials.

Awards: Ribbons to six places and cash awards for the top two places will be presented in two categories: Junior photographers (age 18 & under) and Adult photographers (age 19 & over). Cash awards will be: first place — $50; second place — $25. Prizes will be awarded to the photographer, regardless of who submits the photograph. The contest is open to both professional and amateur photographers.

Competition: International Student Media Festival.

Sponsor: The Association for Educational Communications and Technology International Student Media Festival, AACUPS–2644 Riva Road, Annapolis, MD 21401.

Purpose: To encourage student media production.

Areas: Animation, computer-generated, multimedia, live action, and sequential still images.

Description: More than 200 student entries of seven minutes or less are entered from students representing many states.

Eligibility: Students kindergarten through college.

Important Dates: October 1 is the competition deadline.

Competition Origin: 1980.

Guidelines Availability: Contact the sponsor in April.

Deadline: October 1.

Winner Notification: November.

How to Enter: Write to the sponsor and ask to be placed on the entry form mailing list.

Judging Criteria: Creativity, originality, organization/purpose, continuity/structure, relevance/importance, documentation, use of available resources, clarity, and energy/education.

Awards: Students receive certificates and critiques. Winners can also attend an awards ceremony.

Competition: Reflections Cultural Arts Program.

Sponsor: The National PTA, 330 N. Wabash Ave., Suite 2100, Chicago, IL 60611.

Purpose: To provide opportunities for students in pre–school through the 12th grade to express and share their creative abilities.

Areas: Literature, music, photography, and visual arts.

Description: This competition is designed to give preschool through high school age students opportunities to express and share their creation. Each year works of art are inspired by a theme which is chosen from hundreds of student theme entries.

Eligibility: Any PTA/PTSA in good standing may sponsor the Reflections Program. Students must participate in Reflections through their local PTA/PTSA. The National PTA does not limit the number of entries a student may submit. Local and state PTAs may set limitations at their discretion.

Important Dates: Contact state PTA for dates.

Guidelines Availability: Available from state PTA.

Deadline: Varies for each state.

Winner Notification: Each state president receives a list in May. All participants receive a certificate and letter of congratulation or regret at this time.

How to Enter: State PTAs submit entries to national level.

Awards: The National PTA awards first, second, and third place in each arts area in each grade division. Honorable mentions may be chosen in each art category and grade division. Place winners receive a cash prize ($300, $200, or $100), a certificate, and a book is donated to each of their schools. One outstanding interpretation winner is chosen from the place winners in each arts area (a total of four). These winners receive an expense–paid trip to the National PTA convention with one adult, a $250 scholarship, and a gold–plated Reflections medallion.

Advice: Each entry must be the work of one student. Each student and his or her parent or guardian must sign the affirmation sentence on the Official Entry Form stating that the entry is original.

Competition: Reflections Scholarship Competition.

Sponsor: The National PTA, 330 N. Wabash Ave., Suite 2100, Chicago, IL 60611–3690.

Purpose: To provide scholarships for students wishing to pursue arts in their future education.

Areas: Literature, music, photography, and visual arts.

Description: The Reflections Scholarship Competition consists of four scholarships of $750 each, one in each of four arts areas: literature, music, photography, and visual arts. It is directed toward students who wish to pursue the arts in their future education.

Eligibility: Each student must be a senior in high school.

Important Dates: Deadline for requesting application is the last Friday in November.

Guidelines Availability: Contact sponsor.

Deadline: The deadline for requesting an application is the last Friday in November. After that date applications may be requested from your state PTA office. All requests must include the national ID number for your local PTA unit which can be acquired through your local unit president or state office.

Winner Notification: Announced in March.

How to Enter: Submit two original works. Submit a completed application packet including: a personal essay, completed entry forms (with signed verification from the local PTA president and national ID number for the local PTA unit), and a teacher's letter of recommendation (including recommendation form).

Judging Criteria: Judging criteria include maturity of work, articulation of personal goals in the essay, and teacher's letter of recommendation.

Judges: A jury is assembled from professionals from each arts area.

Awards: Four scholarships of $750 each.

Competition: Toshiba NSTA ExploraVision Awards Program.

Sponsor: National Science Teachers Association, 1840 Wilson Blvd., Arlington, VA 22201.

Purpose: To provide opportunities for K–12 students to enhance or design technologies that could exist in the future.

Area: Futuristic technology design.

Description: This is the world's largest science contest in which teams of three to four students in grades K–12 expand on or design technologies that could exist 20 years in the future.

Eligibility: Open to all students in grades K–12.

Important Dates: February 1 is the entry deadline; in mid–March the 48 regional semi–finalist teams are announced; in mid– April videos are due from the semi–finalists; in the beginning of May the 12 finalist teams are announced and in early June the four first–place winners (one from each grade category) and the eight second–place teams (two from each grade category) are announced at a press conference that is the kick–off to an awards weekend.

Competition Origin: 1992.

Guidelines Availability: Contact the sponsor in September.

Deadline: February 1.

Winner Notification: Winners are notified in early June.

How to Enter: Students participate in teams of three or four with a teacher–advisor and an optional community advisor in one of four grade levels K–3, 4–6, 7–9, and 10–12, must be under 21 years of age, and be a full–time student in an accredited institution. By February 1 the teams must submit a teacher–signed entry form, a 10–page or fewer typed description of their technology, and story boards depicting scenes from a sample five–minute video they would produce to convey their ideas.

Judging Criteria: Decisions are based upon creativity, scientific accuracy, communication, and feasibility of vision.

Judges: Leading science educators serve as judges.

Awards: The 48 regional semi–finalist teams each receive $500 to produce the video for the final judging. Each student who enters and each teacher and community advisor who sponsors a team will receive a certificate of participation and a small gift. The schools of the 48 semi–finalist teams will receive a television and a VCR. The 36 semi–finalist team members who do not go on to the finals each receive a $100 savings bond. Schools of the 12 finalist teams each receive a Toshiba product such as a FAX machine, copier, etc. The teacher advisors of the 12 finalists' teams also receive a Toshiba product. The 12 finalist team members, their teachers, and parents will be given a trip to Washington, DC, in June for the awards ceremony. Student members of the four first–place teams each receive a $10,000 savings bond while the students on the eight second–place teams each receive a $5,000 savings bond.

Competition: Video Voyages Contest.

Sponsor: Weekly Reader Corporation and Panasonic Company, 245 Long Hill Road, P.O. Box 2791, Middletown, CT 06457–9291.

Purpose: To recognize original videos made by teams or classes of elementary and secondary students in grades 5–12.

Area: Videotaping.

Description: Teams or classes of students create and submit original videos.

Eligibility: Grades 5–12.

Competition Origin: 1991.

Guidelines Availability: Contact the sponsor in November.

Deadline: March.

Winner Notification: May.

How to Enter: Contact sponsor.

Judges: Videos are judged by staff members from Weekly Reader Corporation and Panasonic Company.

Awards: Ten winning teams or classes receive a selection of Panasonic video equipment for their schools.

Advice: All entries become the property of Weekly Reader Corporation, and none will be returned. Please write or call for complete contest rules and entry forms.

Visual Arts

Competition: American Morgan Horse Association Morgan Horse Art Contest.

Sponsor: American Morgan Horse Association, P.O. Box 960, Shelbourne, VT 05482–0960.

Purpose: To display artistic abilities in any way you choose.

Areas: Pencil sketches, oils, water colors, paintbrush, sculptures, carvings, embroidery, and other unique styles of Morgan art.

Description: Contest held for the purpose of allowing students to creatively express their knowledge and interest in Morgan Horses.

Eligibility: Junior — up to 17 years of age; Senior — 18 & over; and Professional — commercial artists.

Guidelines Availability: Contact sponsor in early fall.

Deadline: December 1 postmark.

Winner Notification: Upon completion of judging.

How to Enter: Each art piece must be submitted in the following form. Any size, shape, or version of *original* artwork will be accepted. If matting is used, please refrain from spray mounting. The sponsor must be able to remove artwork from matting. Each piece must have its own application form. Each piece must have its own entry fee. Entries must be postmarked by December 1 of each year to be considered for the contest.

Judging Criteria: Artwork will be judged on breed promotion, creativity, artistic quality, and overall appearance. Images must clearly identify the Morgan as a horse breed. You may enter as many times as your creativity will allow. Artwork must be original works of the artist.

Judges: American Morgan Horse Association officials.

Awards: Winners receive the following: Junior: first place — $40 AMHA Catalog certificate; second place — $20 AMHA Gift Catalog certificate; third through fifth place — $10 AMHA Gift Catalog certificate. Senior & Professional: first place — $50 cash; second place — $25 cash; third through fifth — $10 AMHA Gift Catalog certificate. Ribbons are sent to all placings. Other entries will receive Certificate of Participation. Top placings may be used for AMHA logos, clothing designs or on other items with credit given to the artist. A selection of winning art is exhibited at the AMHA headquarters during the tourist season. Artwork is auctioned at the AMHA Annual Convention the following year.

Advice: When shipping your artwork, please be sure it is adequately protected. We cannot be responsible for work which is damaged in transport.

Competition: Arts Recognition and Talent Search (ARTS) Program.

Sponsor: National Foundation for Advancement in the Arts, 800 Brickell Ave., Suite 500, Miami, FL 33131.

Purpose: To recognize young American artists of exceptional ability and provide them with the opportunity to be evaluated by panels of experts in their field, considered for scholarships offered by NFAA's Scholarship List Service subscriber, receive unrestricted cash grants; participate in ARTS Week, be nominated to the White House Commission on Presidential Scholars, and benefit from NFAA's ongoing support of its alumni through various internship and career advancement programs.

Areas: Dance, Music, Music/Jazz, Music/Voice, Theater, Photography, Visual Arts, and Writing.

Description: Of the more than 7,000 high school senior–age artists who apply, approximately 350 will earn ARTS awards. Of that number, 120 will be invited, at NFAA's expense, to participate in "ARTS Week," six full days of judged individual auditions, workshops, master classes, and seminars in Miami, FL. As a result of the "ARTS Week" adjudications, each artist will receive an award in the amount of $3,000, $1,500, $1,000, $500 or $100. The balance of awardees who do not participate in "ARTS Week," but are deemed worthy of recognition, earn $100 honorable mention awards. Up to 50 top ARTS awardees will be nominated by NFAA to the White House Commission on Presidential Scholars for designation as U.S. Presidential Scholars in the Arts, the highest honor bestowed on graduating American high school seniors who excel in the arts. Ultimately, 20 will be chosen for this prestigious award and honored at a White House ceremony during National Recognition Week in June. All students who participate in ARTS are eligible for more than $2 million in scholarship opportunities offered by more than 100 colleges, universities, and professional arts institutions.

Eligibility: If you are enrolled in high school, you must be a senior in the contest's academic year. If you are not enrolled in high school (whether you are enrolled in college, a high school graduate not enrolled in college, or an individual not completing high school), you must be 17-18 years old on December 1. You must be a citizen or permanent resident of the United States or of its official territories.

Important Dates: June 1 — early deadline, non–refundable registration fee required: $25 per discipline or discipline category entered; October 1 — late deadline, non–refundable registration fee required: $35 per discipline or discipline category entered; November 1 — postmark deadline for submission of application packet.

Competition Origin: The National Foundation for Advancement in the Arts was founded in 1981 as an independent, nongovernmental, publicly supported, 501(c)3 national arts organization. It was founded on the premise that investing in the lives and work of promising young artists at critical points in their artistic growth ensures the nation's cultural vitality and enhances life in all its dimensions.

Deadline: June.

Winner Notification: In December, winners are notified of their invitation to Miami for ARTS Week, a week of live adjudications consisting of auditions, master and technique classes, workshops, studio exercises, and interviews. NFAA pays roundtrip airfare within the U.S. and its territories, lodging, and meal expenses.

How to Enter: Complete the ARTS registration form and send it along with appropriate fees. You will then receive a detailed packet of instructions along with a program identification number. Applicants need to read packet information very carefully and follow directions. Packet materials must be postmarked by November 1.

Judging Criteria: The judges, using a two–step process, review materials submitted by the applicants, selecting up to 20 award candidates in each of the eight disciplines (five in Music/Jazz and Music/Voice and 10 in Photography) for live adjudications in Miami. An unlimited amount of $100 Honorable Mention awards are granted to selected applicants who are not invited to Miami.

Judges: Panels of experts — one panel for each art discipline.

Awards: First level awards, $3,000; second level awards, $1,500; third level awards, $1,000; fourth level awards, $500; and fifth level awards, $50.

Competition: Congressional Art Competition.

Sponsor: Congressional Arts Caucus, U.S. Congress, Washington, DC 20515.

Purpose: To afford students the opportunity to express their creativity and to share these creative talents with the community.

Areas: Painting, drawing, collage, and printing.

Description: Students submit artwork based upon a particular theme at the congressional district level with winners competing at the national level.

Eligibility: Open to all students in grades 9–12.

Important Dates: Congressional competitions are announced in the fall and held in the spring.

Competition Origin: 1980.

Guidelines Availability: Contact your local congressional representative.

Deadline: Varies at each level of competition.

How to Enter: Guidelines and entry forms are available from your local congressional representative.

Judging Criteria: Creativity.

Awards: All students receive a certificate signed by a member of Congress. At the district level, winning artwork is displayed for a year in local district offices of congress members. At the national level, winning artwork is displayed for a year in the Cannon Tunnel.

Competition: The Elvis Week Annual Art Exhibit and Contest.

Sponsor: The Elvis Week Annual Art Exhibit and Contest, Graceland, Division of Elvis Presley Enterprises Inc., 3734 Elvis Presley Blvd., Memphis, TN 38116.

Purpose: To provide artists the opportunity to express their feelings and ideas about the rock and roll legend, Elvis Presley.

Area: Visual arts.

Description: The Art Exhibit and Contest offers four judged categories as well as two exhibit only categories. Judged categories are: Craft Division, Non–Professional Art Division, Professional Art Division, and Photography Division. The Exhibit only categories are: Youth Art Division (for ages 16 and under) and Special Division (for disabled artists). Artists who enter the Youth or Special Division may also enter one or more of the other categories. There is no charge to enter the contest.

Eligibility: Open to all youth ages 16 and under.

Important Dates: Artwork is on display (no admission charge) at Graceland in August. Judging for the competing categories is in early August.

Deadline: Entry deadline for art to arrive at Graceland is at the end of July.

Winner Notification: Winners, if not present, will be notified by mail.

How to Enter: For complete rules and entry form, contact sponsor.

Judges: A panel of judges from the Memphis community choose one entry for an Award of Excellence as well as first, second, and third place winners in the judged categories. Fan favorite voting is held in August.

Awards: Winners of the judged categories will receive ribbons and token of appreciation. Each entrant of the Youth and Special Divisions will receive a certificate along with a token of appreciation.

Advice: All art must be the original work of the exhibitors (copies are not accepted) and must relate to the image of Elvis Presley or his home, Graceland.

Competition: *Junior Scholastic* Find the Map Man.

Sponsor: *Junior Scholastic*, 555 Broadway, New York, NY 10012.

Purpose: To encourage students to use the map–reading and geography skills that they have learned in the magazine in competing for prizes and national recognition.

Areas: Map knowledge and map drawing.

Description: Students must find the Map Man by reading two maps and correctly answering questions based on the maps. The correct answers lead students to the mystery location, of which they must then draw a map.

Eligibility: Open to all *Junior Scholastic* readers. The magazine is published for grades 6–8, but it is read by some younger and some older students.

Important Dates: Contest appears in two consecutive November issues. Entries must be postmarked by December 1, and winners are announced in the February issue.

Guidelines Availability: See November issues of *Junior Scholastic*.

Deadline: Postmarked by December 1.

Winner Notification: Winners announced in February issue of *Junior Scholastic*.

How to Enter: Follow directions for entry as described in November issues of *Junior Scholastic*.

Judging Criteria: Entries are judged based upon originality, accuracy, attention to detail, artistic merit, creativity, originality, and execution.

Judges: The person who draws all of the maps appearing in the magazine is the judge.

Awards: The entry with the most correct answers and the best, most original map will win the grand prize of a $500 U.S. Savings Bond. Runners-up receive Map Man T–shirts. Special awards are given to school classrooms that submit the best entries.

Competition: "Kids Helping Kids" Greeting Card Contest.

Sponsor: Co-sponsored by UNICEF, Better Homes and Gardens, and Pier 1; United States Committee for UNICEF, 333 E. 38th St., New York, NY 10016.

Purpose: To allow children the opportunity to depict through artwork the ideal that even though kids come from different countries, they all need the same things to survive and grow.

Areas: Pencil, pen, crayon, color marker, or paint artwork.

Description: Children create greeting cards based upon a theme.

Competition Origin: 1991.

Deadline: Entries are due in late October.

Winner Notification: Notified in early November.

How to Enter: See official contest rules for details.

Judging Criteria: Creativity and quality of expression.

Awards: Two grand prizes are awarded, one each in age groups 7 and under and 8-13. Each grand prize consists of a trip to New York and the United Nations. The two winning cards are printed by the U.S. Committee for UNICEF and sold exclusively at Pier 1 stores.

▼ ▼ ▼ ▼ ▼ ▼ ▼ ▼ ▼ ▼ ▼ ▼ ▼

Competition: The Marie Walsh Sharpe Art Foundation Summer Seminar.

Sponsor: The Marie Walsh Sharpe Art Foundation, 711 N. Tejon, Suite B, Colorado Springs, CO 80903.

Purpose: To offer an intensive visual art studio program for juniors in high school.

Areas: Visual arts.

Description: Students submit an application form with 6–10 copies of at least four individual works, two of which must be drawings, a written statement expressing the most memorable experience of his or her life, and a recommendation from a high school art teacher.

Eligibility: Open to all students who are presently juniors in public and private high schools.

Important Dates: Four two–week sessions each summer.

Competition Origin: 1987.

Deadline: Mid–April.

Winner Notification: Late May.

How to Enter: Contact the sponsor.

Judging Criteria: A panel of jurors designated by the foundation select the participants for the Summer Seminar. The quality and originality of the work represented in the slides of the drawings is the primary criteria for receiving a scholarship. In the final round of deliberations the recommendation and written statement is reviewed for the remaining applicants.

Awards: Full–tuition awards including tuition, room, board, and all seminar–related expenses are provided. Transportation is not included.

▲ ▲ ▲ ▲ ▲ ▲ ▲ ▲ ▲ ▲ ▲ ▲ ▲

Competition: National Writing and Art Contest on the Holocaust.

Sponsor: The United States Holocaust Memorial Museum, 100 Raoul Wallenberg Place S.W., Washington, DC 20024–2150, Attention: National Writing and Art Contest.

Purpose: To invite students to reflect on a topic relating to the Holocaust and to think about the implication for their lives today.

Areas: Art and writing.

Description: For the art contest, students should submit drawings, paintings, and collages. Three–dimensional works are not accepted.

Important Dates: The deadline changes each year; however, it is generally the first week in April.

Competition Origin: The museum has sponsored a National Writing Contest for 10 years, and an Art Contest for two years.

Guidelines Availability: Contact the sponsor.

Deadline: First week in April.

Winner Notification: Winners are notified at the end of May, and the awards ceremony for the winners is in July.

How to Enter: The guidelines for the National Writing and Art Contest are available during the first week of January each year. Teachers should write or call to receive the brochure which includes all information necessary to enter the contest. The topic changes each year so it is important to have the brochure for the current year.

Judging Criteria: Creativity, artistic excellence, and thematic content.

Judges: Museum staff act as the preliminary judges for the contests. After the entries are narrowed to 25 in each category, they are sent to the "official judges." The "official judges" are made up of survivors, historians, artists, writers, museum professionals, and educators throughout the United States who volunteer to judge the contests.

Awards: First place winners are flown to Washington, DC, to visit the United States Holocaust Memorial Museum for a special ceremony. Second place winners receive a framed reproduction of artwork from the United States Holocaust Memorial Museum collection and all winners and their school libraries receive a set of books about the Holocaust and certificates of appreciation. There are prizes for first, second, and third place winners and two honorable mentions.

Advice: Please do not frame or mat the artwork. Photograph the artwork carefully for your portfolio because the Museum does not return entries.

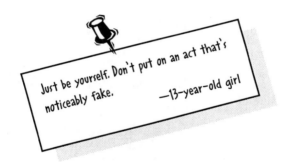

Just be yourself. Don't put on an act that's noticeably fake.
　—13-year-old girl

Competition: National Two–Dimensional Art Contest.

Sponsor: Frances Hook Scholarship Fund, P.O. Box 597346, Chicago, IL 60659–7346.

Purpose: To identify, encourage, and reward promising art students through their participation in a National Two–Dimensional Art Contest.

Area: Two–dimensional art.

Eligibility: Art students in grades 1–12 submit one original two–dimensional art work (photography and sculpture excluded); college undergraduates through age 24 submit three 35mm slides of original art work.

Competition Origin: 1983.

Guidelines Availability: Fall of each year.

Deadline: March 1.

Winner Notification: May 31.

How to Enter: Contact sponsor.

Judges: Independent panel of art teachers, professors, and artists renowned in their respective fields.

Awards: Students vie for $55,000 in scholarship awards given annually.

Competition: *Read* Writing and Art Awards.

Sponsor: *Read* Magazine, Weekly Reader Corp., 245 Long Hill Road, Middletown, CT 06457.

Purpose: To encourage fine creative writing and artwork and to award excellent efforts in same.

Areas: Art, fiction, and essays.

Description: It is a writing and art contest. Winners are published in an all–student–written issue of *Read* in April annually.

Eligibility: 6th–12th grade, males and females, 12–17 years of age.

Important Dates: Mid–December.

Competition Origin: 1979.

Guidelines Availability: Contact the sponsor August through September.

Deadline: Entries must be postmarked no later than mid–December.

Winner Notification: February.

How to Enter: Write to *Read* for full guidelines and entry form contest.

Judging Criteria: Must be original, unpublished, and show true voice, excellent command of English (writing) or materials (art), and a spark and appeal to middle–schoolers.

Judges: Weekly Reader Editorial Staff.

Awards: Prizes are as follows: first — $100 and publication; second — $75; third — $50 in each category. All receive certificates which are excellent for framing.

Advice: Entries must be typed, double-spaced, no longer than six pages, and have an entry coupon stapled or taped to back. Art must have return postage and packing materials if student wants it returned.

Competition: Reflections Cultural Arts Program.

Sponsor: The National PTA, 330 N. Wabash Ave., Suite 2100, Chicago, IL 60611.

Purpose: To provide opportunities for students in pre–school through the 12th grade to express and share their creative abilities.

Areas: Literature, music, photography, and visual arts.

Description: This competition is designed to give pre-school through high school age students opportunities to express and share their creation. Each year works of art are inspired by a theme which is chosen from hundreds of student theme entries.

Eligibility: Any PTA/PTSA in good standing may sponsor the Reflections Program. Students must participate in Reflections through their local PTA/PTSA. The National PTA does not limit the number of entries a student may submit. Local and state PTAs may set limitations at their discretion.

Important Dates: Contact state PTA for dates.

Guidelines Availability: Available from state PTA.

Deadline: Varies for each state.

Winner Notification: Each state president receives a list in May. All participants receive a certificate and letter of congratulation or regret at this time.

How to Enter: State PTAs submit entries to national level.

Awards: The National PTA awards first, second, and third place in each arts area in each grade division. Honorable mentions may be chosen in each art category and grade division. Place winners receive a cash prize ($300, $200, or $100), a certificate, and a book is donated to each of their schools. One outstanding interpretation winner is chosen from the place winners in each arts area (a total of four). These winners receive an expense–paid trip to the National PTA convention with one adult, a $250 scholarship, and a gold–plated Reflections medallion.

Advice: Each entry must be the work of one student. Each student and his or her parent or guardian must sign the affirmation sentence on the Official Entry Form stating that the entry is original.

Competition: Reflections Scholarship Competition.

Sponsor: The National PTA, 330 N. Wabash Ave., Suite 2100, Chicago, IL 60611–3690.

Purpose: To provide scholarships for students wishing to pursue arts in their future education.

Areas: Literature, music, photography, and visual arts.

Description: The Reflections Scholarship Competition consists of four scholarships of $750 each, one in each of four arts areas: literature, music, photography, and visual arts. It is directed toward students who wish to pursue the arts in their future education.

Eligibility: Each student must be a senior in high school.

Important Dates: Deadline for requesting application is the last Friday in November.

Guidelines Availability: Contact sponsor.

Deadline: The deadline for requesting an application is the last Friday in November. After that date applications may be requested from your state PTA office. All requests must include the national ID number for your local PTA unit which can be acquired through your local unit president or state office.

Winner Notification: Announced in March.

How to Enter: Submit two original works. Submit a completed application packet including: a personal essay, completed entry forms (with signed verification from the local PTA president and national ID number for the local PTA unit), and a teacher's letter of recommendation (including recommendation form).

Judging Criteria: Judging criteria include maturity of work, articulation of personal goals in the essay, and teacher's letter of recommendation.

Judges: A jury is assembled from professionals from each arts area.

Awards: Four scholarships of $750 each.

Competition: Tandy Leather Art Scholarship.

Sponsor: Tandy Leather Company, 1400 Everman Parkway, Fort Worth, TX 76104.

Purpose: To provide students an opportunity to create an original work of art made of at least 50 percent leather.

Area: Leather art.

Description: The student must create a "work of art" made of at least 50 percent leather. The item may be flat, free standing, wearable, or functional. Each entry must be accompanied by a written or typed summary of the student's experience. The summary should include information on what the student learned from the experience, how it related to other school subjects and an assessment of leather as an art material. This summary should be 250 words or less.

Eligibility: The student must be a high school senior on schedule to graduate in the spring of the year of competition. The student must have definite plans to attend a college or university in the fall of that same year. This must be verified by the high school where the student is enrolled.

Important Dates: Deadline for application is April.

Guidelines Availability: Late Winter.

Deadline: April 1.

Winner Notification: May 1.

How to Enter: Complete application which is available from sponsor.

Judging Criteria: Originality, workmanship, and the contents of the written summary.

Judges: Tandy Leather personnel and selected art educators

Awards: First Award: $2,000; Second Award: $1,500; Third Award: $1,000; and Fourth Award: $500.

Advice: Students may submit more than one entry. All scholarship entries must be accompanied by a scholarship application.

Competition: The Scholastic Art Awards.

Sponsor: Alliance for Young Artists and Writers Inc., 555 Broadway, 4th Floor, New York, NY 10012.

Purpose: To recognize achievement by young artists .

Areas: Painting, drawing, mixed media, sculpture, ceramics, video, film animation, computer graphics, jewelry textiles, photography, and portfolios.

Description: Nation's largest and longest running awards program for art.

Eligibility: Open to all students in grades 7–12.

Important Dates: Write for complete information by November 1.

Competition Origin: 1923.

Guidelines Availability: Write for guidelines by November 1.

Deadline: Varies depending upon geographical region.

Winner Notification: May.

How to Enter: Write for entry information. Entries must be accompanied by form and follow procedures.

Judging Criteria: Technical proficiency, style, emergence of artist's vision, and originality.

Judges: Panels of nationally recognized artists, arts professionals, and educators.

Awards: Cash awards, special prizes, and scholarships to seniors who submit portfolios.

Advice: Originality is essential to winning.

Competition: "What's In Your Mind?"

Sponsor: Designs for Education, 1033 Battery St., San Francisco, CA 94111.

Purpose: To promote art and design in high schools and art colleges nationwide; to provide a substantial source of alternative funding for these programs; to recognize and reward student achievement in art and design; to provide young people with a forum for expressing themselves visually; and to generate designs to be produced as part of a line of imprinted sportswear (t–shirts, sweatshirts, boxer shorts, baseball caps, etc.) which is manufactured and marketed by Designs for Education.

Areas: Art/Design.

Description: DfE's "What's in Your Mind" program is run in high school art classes and university and college art departments. Most schools spend anywhere from three to six weeks running the program. DfE produces two lines each year (fall and spring) and holds two design programs (fall and spring). The apparel line is sold to department stores and small specialty stores across the U.S.

Eligibility: The program is open to all students at participating high schools and colleges.

Important Dates: Contact sponsor.

Competition Origin: 1993.

Guidelines Availability: Contact local art teacher.

Deadline: DfE runs school program twice a year (fall and spring). Schools are free to participate in one or both programs each year. Specific deadlines can be obtained by writing or calling the above listed address.

Winner Notification: On an on–going basis after the retailer accepts design.

How to Enter: All artwork is submitted in mass through the art teacher. DfE does not accept single entries from individual artists. The student's school must be a DfE participating school. Interested students should contact their art teacher.

Judging Criteria: Preliminary design selection is conducted at voting sessions at local participating schools. The final selection is up to each individual retailer. Designs are incorporated on an on–going basis year round.

Judges: Designs are first tested at local schools and then shown to retailer.

Awards: For each design DfE produces it awards the artist a $200 design fee. Once the design appears as part of the product line, it is tracked at the whole-sale level in terms of the units sold to retailers nationwide. The designers of the top 20 wholesale selling designs receive scholarships ranging from $5,000 to $500. Each product item sold at retail includes a hangtag which features the student's first name, city of origin, the title of their design, and comments by the artist about what their design means to them. All artwork is returned to the student in care of his or her school. All students retain the rights to their artwork.

Competition: Young American Creative Patriotic Art Awards.

Sponsor: Ladies Auxiliary to the VFW, 406 W. 34th St., Kansas City, MO 64111.

Purpose: To encourage high school students to express their artistic talents, demonstrate their patriotism, and at the same time become eligible for funds to further their art education.

Areas: Water color, pencil, pastel, charcoal, tempera, crayon, acrylic, pen–and–ink, or oil on paper or canvas.

Eligibility: Any student, in grades 9–12.

Important Dates: June 1 is the deadline for submission.

Competition Origin: 1978.

Guidelines Availability: Early spring.

Deadline: June 1.

Winner Notification: Displayed at the National Convention in August.

How to Enter: Contact sponsor for application.

Judging Criteria: Each entry will be judged on the originality of concept and patriotism expressed; the content and clarity of ideas; the design, use of color and technique; and the total impact of execution and contrast.

Judges: Selected by Youth Activities Chairman.

Awards: The prizes are: $3,000, first prize; $2,000, second prize; $1,500, third prize; $1,000, fourth prize; and $500, fifth prize. First prize also includes an all–expenses–paid weekend to the American Academy of Achievement honoring youth champions in many fields of endeavor, plus an all–expenses–paid trip to be honored at the next VFW Auxiliary National Convention. First place art will be featured on the November cover of the National VFW Auxiliary Magazine. Winners must use these funds toward their continued art education or for art supplies.

Competition: Wendy's "A Home and Family" Adoption Art Contest.

Sponsor: Wendy's International, P.O. Box 256, 4288 W. Dublin Granville Road, Dublin, OH 43017.

Purpose: To give both adopted children and those awaiting adoption the picture perfect opportunity to share their feelings on what a family means to them.

Areas: Drawing, painting, sketching, and photography.

Description: Children submit a piece of original artwork depicting their feelings about family.

Eligibility: Open to children up to age 18 who have already been adopted or who are available for adoption.

Important Dates: Judging takes place in January.

Competition Origin: 1994.

Guidelines Availability: Contact sponsor in August for guidelines.

Deadline: November 30 is deadline for entry.

Winner Notification: The winner is announced in early February.

How to Enter: Submit artwork following guidelines from the sponsor.

Judges: Dave Thomas, founder of Wendy's Restaurants, judges all entries.

Awards: All participants receive a certificate of merit, a letter from Dave Thomas, and a coupon for one Wendy's Kids Meal.

LEADERSHIP COMPETITIONS

Competitions: All–USA High School Academic Team Competition.

Sponsors: USA Today, 1000 Wilson Blvd., Arlington, VA 22229–0012.

Purpose: To recognize academic excellence and leadership.

Areas: Academics and leadership.

Description: This program was designed to recognize outstanding high school students.

Eligibility: Grades 9–12.

Important Dates: Postmark nominations by late February.

Guidelines Availability: Contact the sponsor.

Deadline: Late February postmark.

Winner Notification: May.

How to Enter: Nomination forms mailed to all high school principals and guidance directors in USA and American schools overseas.

Judging Criteria: Academic excellence and demonstration of leadership are essential.

Awards: Twenty students are named to First Team and each receive a cash award of $2,500 and recognition in *USA TODAY*.

Competition: Discover Card Tribute Award Scholarships.

Sponsor: Discover Card Service Inc. and the American Association of School Administrators, 1801 N. Moore St., Arlington, VA 22209.

Purpose: To award scholarships in recognition of high school juniors who exhibit excellence in many areas of their lives, other than academics.

Areas: Must demonstrate accomplishments in four out of these five areas: (1) Special Talent; (2) Leadership; (3) Unique Endeavors; (4) Community Service; and (5) Obstacles Overcome.

Description: Scholarships for education or training beyond high school, no matter what career path, can be used for coursework, certificate trade schools, associate, or bachelor degrees.

Eligibility: High school juniors — at least 2.75 GPA for ninth and tenth grades.

Guidelines Availability: Available September through December of each year.

Deadline: Mid–January of each year.

Winner Notification: Notified in May by letters to student, principal, and superintendent.

How to Enter: Write to sponsor.

Judging Criteria: Judging based on two–page criteria statement.

Judges: Judging done at state and national level with representatives from business, education, and community.

Awards: Nine awards are given in each state, Washington, DC, and American Schools abroad as follows: three for $1,000, three for $1,500, three for $2,500. Nine national awards are given as follows: three for $10,000, three for $15,000, and three for $20,000.

▼ ▾ ▼ ▾ ▼ ▾ ▼ ▾ ▼ ▾ ▼ ▾ ▼ ▾ ▼ ▾ ▼ ▾

Competition: HOBY Sophomore Leadership Seminars.

Sponsor: Hugh O'Brian Youth Foundation (HOBY), 10880 Wilshire Blvd. #1103, Los Angeles, CA 90024.

Purpose: To seek out, recognize, and develop leadership potential among high school sophomores, and to promote understanding among this group of America's Incentive System.

Areas: Leadership.

Description: Schools select a student who best represents their community's concept of an outstanding sophomore student leader.

Eligibility: All high school sophomores are eligible.

Important Dates: Nomination forms are sent to all high schools in the fall. Forms must have been returned by the high schools to the L.A. office for guaranteed acceptance by mid–November. The final deadline for acceptance is the end of February.

Competition Origin: 1958.

Guidelines Availability: Competition guidelines do not change from year to year.

Deadline: February 28 of each year.

Winner Notification: Responsibility of each school.

How to Enter: Apply to principal and/or guidance counselor.

Judging Criteria: Every high school in the U.S. is mailed a student nomination form. Prospective students are asked to complete three essay questions on the form: How have you: 1) demonstrated leadership ability? 2) expressed sensitivity and concern for others? 3) shown the desire to learn and share knowledge and experience with others?

Judges: Each student applicant's school principal or guidance counselor is the judge. A school "selection panel" may also be formed.

Awards: Upon selection, the student will be allowed to attend one of HOBY's 91 leadership seminars in his or her state free of charge. At this seminar the

△ ▲ △ ▲ △ ▲ △ ▲ △ ▲ △ ▲ △ ▲ △ ▲ △

student will interact with identified leaders in the fields of business, industry, science, arts, education, and government.

Advice: The vast majority of HOBY's work is done through its 4000 volunteers across the U.S., Canada, Mexico, and the Bahamas. There is no cost to the student, school, or parent. HOBY accepts no United Way or government money. From each local leadership seminar, one boy and girl are selected to attend HOBY's week long World Leadership Congress (WLC) in July, at no cost. The WLC is held in a different city each year and is coordinated by a major university.

▽ ▽ ▽ ▽ ▽ ▽ ▽ ▽ ▽ ▽ ▽ ▽ ▽

Competition: I Dare You Leadership Award.

Sponsor: I Dare You Leadership Award, 1315 Ann Ave., St. Louis, MO 63104.

Purpose: To recognize the leadership capacity of high school students and 4–H participants.

Areas: Leadership.

Description: Students apply for I Dare You Leadership Awards. Recipients of the awards are eligible for a scholarship to the International Leadership Conference. The program is intended to focus on "emerging" leaders — those young adults who have the qualities and abilities to lead, but who may not yet recognize or act on their leadership potential.

Eligibility: The program is directed to high school juniors and 4–H participants. They should demonstrate personal integrity, lead well–rounded lives, and possess a willingness to assume responsibility. They do not need to hold leadership positions currently, but be recognized by their peers and adults who work with them as emerging leaders.

Important Dates: Conference registration due March 15.

Competition Origin: The I Dare You Leadership Award was first offered in 1941 by William H. Danforth.

Deadline: March 15.

Winner Notification: Prior to June 1.

How to Enter: Complete selection form provided by sponsor.

Judging Criteria: Recognition by peers and adults who work with students serving as emerging leaders.

Judges: American Youth Foundation officials.

Awards: The I Dare You Leadership Award consists of three elements: A personalized award certificate, a copy of I Dare You!, eligibility to apply for a scholarship to the International Leadership Conferences.

Advice: Scholarships awarded on a first–come, first–serve basis.

△ △ △ △ △ △ △ △ △ △ △ △ △ △

Competition: Freedoms Foundation National Awards Program.

Sponsor: Freedoms Foundation, Valley Forge, Rt. 23, Valley Forge, PA 19482–0706.

Purpose: To publicly honor and recognize the exceptional efforts of individuals, organizations, corporations, and schools who promote, through words or deeds, an understanding of responsible citizenship and the benefits of a free society.

Areas: Most youth category entries are in the form of written essays and speeches. However, projects for individual achievement or involvement in the communities are also welcome.

Description: Eligible material must have been written, developed or released during the May 1 to April 30 awards year.

Eligibility: Open to all citizens and legal residents of the U.S. grades K–12.

Important Dates: May 1 is deadline for entry. Award ceremonies are conducted by regional Volunteer Chapters beginning October 15.

Competition Origin: 1949.

Guidelines Availability: Year–round.

Deadline: May 1 of each year.

Winner Notification: Awardees will be announced by September 1 of each year.

How to Enter: Submit typed copy of essay or speech. Activities should be put in a ring binder or scrap book with substantiating materials.

Judging Criteria: A nomination must relate to one or more of the basic American rights set forth in the *American Credo* or the obligations outlined in the *Bill of Responsibilities*.

Judges: National Awards Jury is comprised of chief and associate State Supreme Court justices, executive offices from National Veteran Service and civic clubs, veterans, or educational organizations.

Awards: Top recipient in Youth Category receives $100 U.S. Saving Bond and framed George Washington Honor Medal. All other recipients receive George Washington Honor Medal.

Advice: Winning entries from other local/national contests are eligible. Entries may not be the product of classroom assignments.

Competition: National Society Daughters of the American Revolution Good Citizens Contest.

Sponsor: National Society Daughters of the American Revolution, 1776 D St. N.W., Washington, DC 20006–5392.

Purpose: To encourage and reward the qualities of good citizenship.

Area: Citizenship.

Description: The DAR Good Citizens Scholarship Contest consists of two parts. Part I (Personal) is a series of questions asking the student to describe how he or she has tried to manifest the qualities of a Good Citizen. This part may be completed at home and is to be submitted together with a copy of his or her scholastic record and one letter of recommendation. Part II (Essay) is to be administered under the supervision of faculty or DAR member. It must be completed at one sitting, within a two–hour time limit, and without assistance or reference materials. Part I and Part II each represent half of the total contest entry score. Each contest entry is evaluated by independent judges with the first place entry automatically forwarded on to the next level of judging until, ultimately, the final entries are judged on the national level and the national winners are selected.

Eligibility: Males and females may both enter. Program is open to all senior class students enrolled in accredited public or private secondary schools or secondary schools which are in good standing with their state board of education. U.S. citizenship is not a requirement.

Important Dates: DAR national vice chairs shall have state winner contest entries judged and all first place division winner entries should be sent to national chair by mid–February.

Competition Origin: 1934.

Guidelines Availability: Information can be obtained through the DAR chairman in your state.

Deadline: Mid–February.

Winner Notification: Winners are notified by March 10th.

How to Enter: Contact DAR Good Citizen chair of the state in which you live.

Judging Criteria: Must have qualities of dependability, service, leadership, and patriotism.

Judges: The State Society DAR and the State Department of Education determine the method of selection of the State DAR Good Citizen. School DAR Good Citizen: Each school chooses its own student for this honor.

Awards: The national awards are as follows: First place winner: $5,000 scholarship; second place winner: $2,000; third place winner, $1,000. Each state and division winner receives $250.

Advice: Each chapter chairman should obtain the cooperation of the school administration as soon as possible so that DAR Good Citizen program contest may be included in the schedule.

Competition: Presidential Classroom.

Sponsor: A Presidential Classroom for Young Americans Inc., 119 Oronoco St., Alexandria, VA 22314.

Purpose: To help prepare outstanding high school juniors and seniors for leadership and civic responsibility by providing firsthand exposure to the federal government in action.

Areas: Leadership and civics.

Description: Each of the one–week sessions in Washington, DC, gives students an "inside" view of government and the American political process. Students meet with and question the country's most influential leaders, discuss issues with peers from across the U.S. and abroad, and visit the historic sites of our nation's capitol. Students renew their self–confidence, gain a broader understanding of government, and continue to build their leadership credentials.

Eligibility: Students must be high school juniors or seniors (rising juniors may attend summer sessions); maintain at least a B average or rank in the top 25 percent of their class; and submit the authorization of their school principal.

Competition Origin: Incorporated in 1968.

Guidelines Availability: Year–round.

Deadline: Registration deadlines of December 1 and May 1 scholarship applications due mid–November.

Winner Notification: Upon receipt and acceptance of application.

How to Enter: Complete application process.

Judging Criteria: See eligibility requirements. Those interested in scholarship opportunities must demonstrate genuine financial need; maintain at least a 3.8 grade point average; and hold leadership positions in school or community organizations.

Judges: Presidential Classroom Staff.

Awards: Limited scholarships available.

Competition: United States Senate Youth Program.

Sponsor: William Randolph Hearst Foundation, 90 New Montgomery St. #1212, San Francisco, CA 94105–4505.

Purpose: To encourage leadership qualities and an interest in government and community service.

Areas: Leadership, service, and government.

Description: The selection process varies by state — the department of education of each state handles the selection process for the foundation.

Eligibility: High school juniors or seniors who are currently serving as elected student body officers are eligible. Students must be permanent residents of state where parents legally reside.

Competition Origin: 1962.

Guidelines Availability: Information can be requested year–round.

Deadline: Early Fall — varies by state.

Winner Notification: Generally, first week of December.

How to Enter: Contact high school principal, state department of education, or call foundation for department of education information.

Judging Criteria: Varies by state.

Awards: 104 $2,000 college scholarships and all-expenses-paid week in Washington, DC.

Advice: Students should start exploring participation in this program soon after school year begins.

Competition: Youth Salute.

Sponsor: National Council On Youth Leadership, 689 Craig Road, Suite 10, St. Louis, MO 63141.

Purpose: To assist communities to applaud, encourage, and develop leadership skills of their youth.

Areas: Leadership.

Description: High school juniors are nominated by their high schools to the local NCYL chapter early spring. Nominating criteria are: B grade average, elected to a leadership position by their peers in the past two years, and good citizen. Students meeting these criteria receive community recognition through photo displays and are invited to a local leadership workshop. Community representatives then review students' applications and select two students to attend NCYL's national leadership conference, held in St. Louis, MO, each October.

Eligibility: High school juniors.

Competition Origin: 1980.

Guidelines Availability: Continuous.

Deadline: October 1 for selected students to register for national conference.

How to Enter: There is no open application process. You must be in a community which has or will start an NCYL chapter.

Judging Criteria: Balanced accomplishments in school and community, and leadership skills essay.

Judges: Various community representatives.

Awards: Communities frequently award college scholarships based on available funds. Two students are invited from each community to attend NCYL's national leadership conference at no cost.

▽ ▽ ▽ ▽ ▽ ▽ ▽ ▽ ▽ ▽ ▽ ▽ ▽

Competition: Yoshiyama Award for Exemplary Service to the Community.

Sponsor: The Yoshiyama Award, P.O. Box 19247, Washington, DC 20036–9247.

Purpose: To recognize high school seniors who have distinguished themselves through extensive service and leadership in their communities.

Areas: Service and leadership.

Description: This award is given annually to six to ten high school seniors selected from throughout the United States on the basis of their community service activities.

Eligibility: Graduating and rising high school seniors.

Important Dates: Nomination packets must be postmarked April 1.

Competition Origin: 1988.

Guidelines Availability: Contact sponsor.

Deadline: April 1.

Winner Notification: August or September.

How to Enter: Complete the nomination form, letter of nomination, and two supporting letters.

Judging Criteria: Community service, self–motivation, leadership, creativity, dedication, and commitment.

Judges: National panel of outstanding leaders, representing various professions, but all committed to the development of leadership and civic responsibility.

Awards: $5,000 gift, dispensed over two years, to be used at the discretion of award recipients and an invitation to a special award ceremony and retreat in Washington, DC.

Advice: Students may not nominate themselves.

▲ ▲ ▲ ▲ ▲ ▲ ▲ ▲ ▲ ▲ ▲ ▲ ▲

SERVICE LEARNING COMPETITIONS

Competition: A Pledge and A Promise Environmental Awards.

Sponsor: Education Department, Sea World, 7007 Sea World Drive, Orlando, FL 32821.

Purpose: To recognize the outstanding efforts of school groups in the areas of environmental awareness and action.

Areas: Environmental science and service.

Description: These awards are primarily service–oriented with some academics included. The awards focus on the actions school groups take to help protect the planet's natural resources.

Eligibility: All school ages are eligible to apply for these awards. They are not gender specific. The four categories are: K–5, 6–8, 9–12, and college.

Important Dates: Applications are available in September and are due by January 30.

Deadline: January 30.

Winner Notification: Winner notification occurs in the spring (date varies).

How to Enter: School groups within these categories can enter the A Pledge and A Promise Environmental Awards by submitting the environmental projects they have completed or works in progress to better the planet around them.

Judging Criteria: Several criteria are considered by the judges. They consider the projects based on their creativity, innovation, measurable effects, benefits to the community, and benefits to the environment. The judges will examine whether the projects are transferable. That is, do they serve as a model for other groups to imitate and implement. Also, they will consider whether the projects offer a long–term gain for the environment and community. Other criteria considered are that the projects be developed and implemented prior to the application deadline and that they be student–driven.

Judges: The judges for the competition are representatives from several environmental organizations. These include: Center for Marine Conservation, Hubbs–Sea World Research Institute, the Izaak Walton League of America, the National Fish and Wildlife Federation, the National Wildlife Federation, and the Sea World/Busch Gardens Education Departments.

Awards: Cash awards are presented for these environmental projects. A total of 13 given across the four categories. In each age category, the following awards are presented: first place — $12,500; second place — $5,000; third place — $2,500. A grand prize of $20,000 is awarded to the one project that is judged the overall best in any category. All awards are made on behalf of and for the advancement of the school group's project.

Advice: It is critical that the application be completed accurately and that the project is creative and student–driven.

Competition: Discover Card Tribute Award Scholarships.

Sponsor: Discover Card Service Inc. and the American Association of School Administrators, 1801 N. Moore St., Arlington, VA 22209.

Purpose: To award scholarships in recognition of high school juniors who exhibit excellence in many areas of their lives other than just academics.

Areas: Must demonstrate accomplishments in four out of these five areas: (1) Special Talent; (2) Leadership; (3) Unique Endeavors; (4) Community Service; and (5) Obstacles Overcome.

Description: Scholarships for education or training beyond high school no matter what career path; can be used for coursework, certificate trade schools, associate, or bachelor degrees

Eligibility: High school juniors — at least 2.75 GPA for 9th and 10th grades.

Guidelines Availability: Available September through December of each year.

Deadline: Mid–January of each year.

Winner Notification: Notified in May by letters to student, principal, and superintendent.

How to Enter: Write to sponsor.

Judging Criteria: Judging based on two–page criteria statement.

Judges: Judging done at state and national level with representatives from business, education, and community.

Awards: Nine awards are given in each state, Washington, DC, and American Schools abroad as follows: three for $1,000, three for $1,500, three for $2,500. Nine national awards are given as follows: three for $10,000, three for $15,000, and three for $20,000.

Competition: Firestone Firehawks.

Sponsor: Bridgestone/Firestone Inc., 50 Century Blvd., Nashville, TN 37219.

Purpose: To recognize children between the ages of 5 and 15 for their efforts on behalf of the environment.

Area: Environmental advocacy.

Description: Children are inducted into the Firehawks club (receive T–shirts and other memorabilia), and have the opportunity to win an all–expenses–paid trip to Olympic National Park in Washington.

Eligibility: All children, 5 to 15 years old.

Important Dates: The trip is scheduled for July each year.

Competition Origin: 1991.

Guidelines Availability: Requests for applications are accepted year-round. Application forms are printed in January and sent to all who have made requests since the last contest.

Deadline: Mid–April.

Winner Notification: Mid–May.

How to Enter: The application form requires vital information as well as supporting information about the environmental program.

Judging Criteria: Activity versus age abilities, the number of people served by the activity, and the duration of the activity.

Judges: Bridgestone/Firestone and an independent panel of judges are selected each year.

Awards: Club memorabilia, all–expenses–paid excursion to Olympic National Park for Environmental Education.

Competition: JC Penney Golden Rule Award and National Golden Rule Awards.

Sponsor: JC Penney in a co–partnership with Volunteer Centers or United Ways across the country in more than 200 markets. For more information write to JC Penney Golden Rule Award, P.O. Box 10001, Dallas, TX 75301–8101.

Purpose: To recognize, honor, and reward outstanding volunteer efforts through a reception, Waterford Crystal statue, and a $1,000 donation to the non–profit organization they serve.

Area: Volunteer service only.

Description: Nominations are solicited and then judges who are civic and community leaders select a youth winner among several other categories.

Eligibility: Must be 18 years or younger at time of nomination — male or female.

Important Dates: Each local program has a different deadline for nominations.

Competition Origin: Youth award was added to existing program in 1989.

Winner Notification: Decided by local JC Penney Store.

How to Enter: Nominations are in most non–profits and schools where program is available.

Judges: JC Penney and co–partner in each community where program exists invites community leaders to be judges.

Awards: Waterford Crystal Award and $1,000 contribution as a local winner and a potential to win National Golden Rule Award which would include an additional contribution up to $5,000 and a $5,000 scholarship.

Advice: Nominate yourself or someone you know.

Competition: The Kids' Hall of Fame.

Sponsor: Pizza Hut Inc., P.O. Box 428, Wichita, KS 67201.

Purpose: To recognize kids who have made, or are making, a positive difference.

Areas: Service.

Description: Twenty–five to 100 words are submitted on the nominee and how they made a difference. This difference may be for themselves, their family, their school, their community, their state, their country, or the world.

Eligibility: Age 14 or under.

Important Dates: March 15.

Competition Origin: 1995.

Guidelines Availability: Early fall.

Deadline: March 15.

Winner Notification: Prize winners will be notified of their prize level by phone and/or mail service on or about May 25. With winners' permission, public announcement of winners will be announced via press release on or before June 15.

How to Enter: Complete nomination form and forward.

Judging Criteria: Nominations will be evaluated on the basis of the contribution made by the nominee as measured by the following standards and weighted according to the following percentages: 1) uniqueness of nominee's project in his or her area of contribution (35 percent); 2) the impact that the nominee has made in his or her area of contribution (35 percent); 3) the level of commitment the nominee has exhibited in his or her area of contribution (10 percent); 4) the level of responsibility that the nominee has assumed or achieved in his or her area of contribution (10 percent); and 5) the level of success the nominee has achieved in his or her area of contribution (10 percent). Additionally, to qualify, nominees must have at least a "C" average (or equivalent), meet state mandated school attendance standards, and have no formal criminal record.

Judges: Independent selection panel.

Awards: Five national grand–prize winners will each receive a $10,000 post–high school educational scholarship and a trip to Washington, DC, for themselves and two parents or guardians. Twenty–five first–prize winners will each receive a $100 U.S. Savings Bond.

Competition: President's Environmental Youth Awards.

Sponsor: U.S. Environmental Protection Agency, 401 M St. S.W., Washington, DC 20104.

Purpose: To offer young people an opportunity to become an environmental force within their community.

Areas: Environmental issues and service.

Description: The program has two components: the regional certificate program and the national awards competition. Students are recognized for their efforts to make and keep the world around us a safer, cleaner place to live.

Eligibility: Open to all age groups. Students may compete as individuals, school classes, schools, summer camps, public interest groups, and youth organizations.

Important Dates: Regional applications are accepted year round; however, at the national level, applications must be submitted by July 31.

Guidelines Availability: Contact your regional EPA office for guidelines which are available year–round.

Deadline: July 31.

How to Enter: Obtain an application and detailed guidelines from your regional EPA office.

Judging Criteria: The judging panel considers the following: environmental need for the project; environmental appropriateness of the project, accomplishment of goals, long–term environmental benefits derived from the project; positive environmental impact on the local community and society; evidence of the young person's initiative, innovation, soundness of approach, rationale, and scientific design (if applicable); and clarity and effectiveness of presentation.

Judges: Judging panel selected by the EPA.

Awards: All participants at the regional level receive certificates signed by the president of the United States honoring them for their efforts in environmental protection. The national winners, along with one project sponsor, receive an all–expenses–paid trip to Washington, DC, where they participate in the annual National Awards Ceremony and consult with the EPA Youth Work Group about the program. They also receive a $1,000 grant from Keebler Company. Church & Dwight Company Inc., makers of Arm & Hammer Baking Soda, hosts a luncheon and presents an additional $1,000 grant to each winner, as well as a smaller grant to the first, second, and third place runners–up in each region.

Advice: Contact your regional EPA.

Competition: United States Senate Youth Program.

Sponsor: William Randolph Hearst Foundation, 90 New Montgomery St. #1212, San Francisco, CA 94105–4505.

Purpose: To encourage leadership qualities and an interest in government and community service.

Areas: Leadership, service, and government.

Description: The selection process varies by state — the department of education of each state handles the selection process for the foundation.

Eligibility: High school juniors or seniors who are currently serving as elected student body officers. Students must be permanent residents of state where their parents or legal guardians legally reside.

Competition Origin: 1962.

Guidelines Availability: Information can be requested year–round.

Deadline: Early fall — varies by state.

Winner Notification: Generally, first week of December.

How to Enter: Contact high school principal, state department of education, or call foundation for department of education information.

Judging Criteria: Varies by state.

Awards: 104 $2,000 college scholarships and all-expenses-paid week in Washington, DC.

Advice: Students should start exploring participation in this program soon after the school year begins.

Competition: Yoshiyama Award for Exemplary Service to the Community.

Sponsor: The Yoshiyama Award, P.O. Box 19247, Washington, DC 20036–9247.

Purpose: To recognize high school seniors who have distinguished themselves through extensive service and leadership in their communities.

Areas: Service and leadership.

Description: This award is given annually to six to ten high school seniors selected from throughout the United States on the basis of their community service activities.

Eligibility: Graduating and rising high school seniors.

Important Dates: Nomination packets must be postmarked April 1.

Competition Origin: 1988.

Guidelines Availability: Contact sponsor.

Deadline: April 1.

Winner Notification: August or September.

How to Enter: Complete the nomination form, letter of nomination, and two supporting letters.

Judging Criteria: Community service, self–motivation, leadership, creativity, dedication, and commitment.

Judges: National panel of outstanding leaders, representing various professions, but all committed to the development of leadership and civic responsibility.

Awards: $5,000 gift, dispensed over two years, to be used at the discretion of award recipients and an invitation to a special award ceremony and retreat in Washington, DC.

Advice: Students may not nominate themselves.

COMPETITIONS JOURNAL

Why I Want to Enter a Competition

Think of the many great reasons you want to enter competitions! List them and keep them in mind throughout your preparation and participation in competitions.

-
-
-
-
-
-
-
-
-
-
-
-
-
-
-

Top 10 Competitions I'd Like To Be Involved In

What competitions interest you? In which competitions can you see your-self as a terrific participant? Choose your top 10 competitions and list them in rank order from your most favorite to your least favorite. As you begin com-peting you can change your list!

1.

2.

3.

4.

5.

6.

7.

8.

9.

10.

Letter To Obtain Competition Information

From time to time you may hear of additional competitions or need more information on a specific one. A short letter requesting the details will usually get a quick reply. This sample letter will serve as a guide for you.

Date
Your Name and Address

Competitions of Competitions
1000 Competition Street
Competition City, Competition 00000

Dear _____,

    The _____competition is of interest to me
            (NAME)
and I would like more information. Please send materials on the

purpose, requirements, and awards. My name and address are:

    Thank you for responding to this request.

Sincerely yours,

Your name

My Competition Goals

What are your competition goals? In which competitions would you like to be involved? What skills would you like to sharpen? With whom would you like to meet and share your ideas? Competitions can lead to the accomplishment of many personal goals. Find a nice quiet place to sit and think about your goals and how you plan to achieve them through competitions. Write down your thoughts. As you meet your goals, decide on new ones!

GOAL:

STEPS TO ACHIEVING MY GOAL:

1.

2.

3.

4.

5.

GOAL:

STEPS TO ACHIEVING MY GOAL:

1.

2.

3.

4.

5.

The Spirit of Competition!

Think about the spirit of competition ... specifically yours! How do you feel or think you will feel before, during, and after a competition? Write down the ways you feel and the causes of those feelings.

Before a competition, I may
feel or have felt ...

During a competition, I may
feel or have felt ...

After a competition, I may
feel or have felt ...

Things I can do to make myself
feel better ...

How I Selected a Competition
(or better yet, competitions!)

Reflect upon the process you went through in order to select a competition in which you want to participate or have done so. List the many reasons in your selection. You may want to add to this list with each new competition you enter.

My Talents and Abilities:

My Interests:

My Resources:

The Guidelines:

Awards:

Other:

Time Management Tips

As you begin planning for and participating in competitions, you'll quickly find the importance and value of managing your time well. You can do it by following these tips. As you learn to manage your time, write down what works for you ... your very own time management tips.

- *Set priorities.* Decide what is the most important task and do it first. It may help to write down your goals in order of importance.

- *Be flexible.* Remember, some times things change. Take advantage of opportunities to try something different.

- *Plan time to get organized.* Just getting organized takes a few minutes. Grab your calendar, list of goals, and competition information; find a comfortable place to sit; and start organizing and planning.

- *Use little bits of time.* There are times you can use to complete small jobs ... like waiting on the bus, TV commercial breaks during your favorite show, or in between classes. Find something small and get it done.

- *Set deadlines.* Decide when you'd like to have your goals met. Be sure to check off each one as you complete it. And if you finish before a deadline ... good for you!

- *Make and use lists.* Write down your plans for getting ready for the competition. As you finish each step, celebrate by marking it off.

- *Use calendars or appointment books.* These are super tools for staying on top of things. A sample calendar is given in this book. Use it or one of your own.

- *My Time Management Tips.*
    -
    -
    -

My Competition Calendar

Keeping important dates straight is one of the keys to success in competition. Depending upon your individual style and preference, a calendar of some sort will help you do just that. There are pocket calendars and wall calendars, weekly calendars and monthly calendars ... perhaps you have a program in your computer with a calendar. Select the one that's best for you.

Here's a sample:

DAY OF WEEK   THINGS TO DO TODAY

SUNDAY

MONDAY

TUESDAY

WEDNESDAY

THURSDAY

FRIDAY

SATURDAY

▼ ▼ ▼ ▼ ▼ ▼ ▼ ▼ ▼ ▼ ▼ ▼

Things I Need for the Competition

As you prepare for a competition, think about the items you will need for success. List the items you will need, marking those you have and those you will have to acquire. Determine where you will get those items you don't yet have.

Items required:	I have these:	I'll have to get these from:
•	•	•
•	•	•
•	•	•
•	•	•
•	•	•
•	•	•
•	•	•
•	•	•
•	•	•
•	•	•
•	•	•

▲ ▲ ▲ ▲ ▲ ▲ ▲ ▲ ▲ ▲ ▲ ▲ ▲ ▲

Phone Calls

The telephone can be a great tool for asking questions and finding answers, networking with others, and sharing good news. It's important to use good phone manners. Plan your conversation and be certain to write down any important information you receive. This phone form may help you.

"Hello, My name is _____. May I
                              (your name)

please speak to _____ or someone who can
              (name of person)

give me information about the _____
                                (name of competition)

competition?"

What is the purpose in this call? Write what you're going to say or ask.

What information did you receive? Write what you are told by your contact.

"Thank you very much!"

Be sure to write the date and time of the call, as well as the name and phone number of the person with whom you spoke.

Date and Time: _____

Contact Person's Name: _____

Contact Person's Phone Number:_____

Sponsor, Sponsor ... Who's Got a Sponsor?

Competitions sometimes require a school or community sponsor. Other times, sponsors can be located to give support in terms of advice, money, and/or time and goods/services. But how do you get a sponsor? It's easy. Just follow these steps!

- Gather all the facts and details about the competition in which you are interested. Read about it. Be sure you clearly understand the competition.

- Write exactly why you need a sponsor and what you need the sponsor to do. Think about what you will say when you speak to the potential sponsor. You might even want to practice the conversation with someone else.

- Brainstorm individuals or businesses in your school and community who may be willing and able to help you. You may want to ask your parents, teachers, or friends to assist you as you put together this list.

- You may want to look in the yellow pages of your telephone directory or call the local Chamber of Commerce for possible sponsors.

- Contact the sponsor by phone or a letter. Ask if you can set up an appointment or special time to meet so that you can discuss your competition plans and ideas.

- Go visit your sponsor. Be sure you are on time and look nice. Manners are important, too ... so use only the best! Notes and information about the competition may be helpful, so take them. You might want to have an extra copy to leave with the possible sponsor. Smile!

- Be sure to thank your sponsor. A little thanks goes a long way. Remember to let them know how much you enjoyed being a part of the contest in which you entered. Write a thank you note with details of the competition you were able to enter with their help.

Great Lessons I've Learned ...

Competitions can teach us a lot of things about ourselves, our interests, our strengths, and our abilities. We can learn more about our work habits, attitudes, and goals for the future as we meet others, plan projects, and have fun. Think about the great lessons you will or have learned about competitions.

Through competition I will learn more about ...

My interests

My strengths

My abilities

My attitudes

My work habits

My goals

Through competition I have learned more about ...

My interests

My strengths

My abilities

My attitudes

My work habits

My goals

My List Of Recognitions

There are many different kinds of recognition given for participation in competitions. You may receive a medal, trophy, certificate, money, or even a trip. What types of recognition would you like to receive ... or better yet, how have you already been recognized?

List of Recognitions I Would
Like to Receive ...

List of Recognitions I Have
Already Received ...

*

*

*

*

*

*

*

*

*

*

My Slogan For Competitions

What are your feelings and attitudes about competitions? Sum it all up in a slogan. Write a catchy, creative slogan for competitions. Share your ideas with others through a poster, T–shirt design, bumper sticker, play ... the possibilities are endless.

How Did I Do?

In a competition you may be judged by a variety of people ... teachers, trained judges, civic and business leaders, or friends. Have you ever thought about evaluating your own performance? Use the scale below as a tool for discovering your strengths and abilities. Once you've completed it, use the results for your planning and participation in future contests.

****

Rate your performance in a competition!

	Excellent	Good	Average	Fair	Poor
Planning	5	4	3	2	1
Organization	5	4	3	2	1
Time Management	5	4	3	2	1
Participation	5	4	3	2	1
Interactions With Others	5	4	3	2	1
Product	5	4	3	2	1
Attitude	5	4	3	2	1
Appearance	5	4	3	2	1

Competitions Are Fun

Planning and participating in competitions will involve work, but also you'll have tons of fun. You will use your mind in new ways, learn to develop a variety of products, meet new friends, develop and enhance your personal and social skills, and perhaps travel to new and different places. Keeping these memories of all the fun activities will be great. Perhaps you'll want to share these exciting experiences with your friends through discussions, letters, E–mail, editorials in your school or local newspaper, a TV or radio interview, or a dozen other ways.

WAYS I'VE HAD FUN THROUGH COMPETITIONS

•

•

•

•

•

•

•

•

•

•

•

•

▼ ▼ ▼ ▼ ▼ ▼ ▼ ▼ ▼ ▼ ▼ ▼

Being Recognized

Being in competitions may bring recognition to you, your school, and your community. A great way to share your accomplishments is through a press release to be sent to newspapers, television, and/or radio. Look in your local telephone book for the addresses. You may use the format below to notify others of your accomplishments.

PRESS RELEASE

_____ participated in the _____ on _____
    (your name)   (competition)   (date)

in _____. _____is a ___ grade student at _____
 (city, state) (He/She)   (your school)

school in _____. The _____ is designed to
         (city, state)   (competition)

enhance _____.
     (purpose of competition)

You can add more information as you see fit.

▲ ▲ ▲ ▲ ▲ ▲ ▲ ▲ ▲ ▲ ▲ ▲ ▲ ▲

Thank You Letter

Thank you letters are a great way to show your appreciation to the many people who have been encouraging and supportive of you entering a competition. You may want to write to your teacher, sponsor, parents, friends and others. Don't forget to say kind words to the people who were responsible for running the competition. They have worked hard to make it a great event.

Here is a sample thank you note. You'll want to use your own special way of saying your appreciation.

Date
Your Name and Address

Competition of Competitions
1000 Competition Street
Competition City, Competition 00000

Dear ___,

Thank you for the opportunity to participate in the

_____ competition. I learned many new concepts and
  (NAME)
skills. You were very helpful and I appreciate everything you

did.

Sincerely yours,

Your name

What Else Is Out There?

There are many opportunities available for you to share your talents and abilities through competitions. We've given you quite a few national ones from which to chose, but there may be others you'd like to try. As you discover local, regional, state, and national contests of interests, record the information. Share your new ideas with your friends.

Competition: _____

Contact Person: _____

Address: _____

Area of Competition: _____

Date: _____

Competition: _____

Contact Person: _____

Address: _____

Area of Competition: _____

Date: _____

*Your computer can be a useful tool to help you keep up with this information. Create a database file for competitions.

Start a Competition Club

Wouldn't it be fun to share your successes and good ideas with your friends? Why not start a Competition Club? You and your fellow members can share information about upcoming contests, discuss the ups and downs of competing, and best of all, form a network of friends. Before starting your club, think about the following questions.

What will be the purpose of your club?

Who will be able to join your club?

How will new members join?

When and where will your club meet?

Who will help you get your club started?

How will you let others know about your club?

How will you obtain permission to start a club, if indeed permission is needed?

How will you keep the club going?

Will you charge a membership fee?

Let's Hear From You!

You are important to us and we would like to hear from you with your ideas and comments about this book and your participation in competitions. We encourage you to write to us.

I am a:
- ❏ student
- ❏ teacher
- ❏ guidance counselor
- ❏ school administrator
- ❏ competition director
- ❏ other _____

1. What is your favorite competition(s) and why?

2. What have you learned by participating competition(s)?

3. If you have participated in national competitions other than the ones listed in this book, please share the information.

_____

Name of Competition

_____

Address

_____

City, State, Zip

4. What suggestions do you have for additional information for this book?

5. Other comments

****

Mail this form to:
Dr. Frances A. Karnes
University of Southern Mississippi
Box 8207
Hattiesburg, MS 39406–8207

RESOURCES

PHOTOGRAPHY

Ancona, G. (1992). *My camera*. New York, NY: Crown Books for Young Readers.

Evans, A. (1993). *First photos: How kids can take great pictures*. Redondo Beach, CA: Photo Data Resources.

Gleason, R. (1992). *Seeing for yourself: Techniques and projects for beginning photographers*. Chicago, IL: Chicago Review.

Jeunesse, G. (1993). *The camera: Snapshots, movies, videos, and cartoons*. New York, NY: Scholastic Incorporated.

Langford, M. (1993). *Starting photography*. Stoneham, MA: Focal Press.

Marsh, C. (1994). *Hot shot: Photography for kids*. Atlanta, GA: Gallopade Publishing Group.

Morgan, T. & Thaler, S. (1991). *Photography: Take your best shot*. Minneapolis, MN: Lerner Publishings.

Stokes. (1992). *The photography book*. New York, NY: Scholastic Incorporated.

Wilson, K. (1994). *Photography*. New York, NY: Knopf Books for Young Readers.

SPEECHES

Carratello, P. (1981). *I can give a speech*. Westminster, CA: Teacher Created Materials.

Cocetti, R. A. & Snyder, L. (1992). *Talk that matters: An introduction to public speaking*. Kearney, NE: Education Systems Association, Incorporated.

Detz, J. (1986). *You mean I have to stand up and say something?* New York, NY: Macmillan Children's Group.

Dunbar, R. E. (1990). *Making your point*. New York, NY: Watts.

McCutcheon, R. (1993). *Communication matters*. Saint Paul, MN: West Publication.

VISUAL ARTS

Arnold, T. (1986). *My first drawing book*. New York, NY: Workman Publication.

Barish, W. (1983). *I can draw horses*. New York, NY: S&S Trade.

Barry, J. (1990). *Draw, design and paint*. Carthage, IL: Good Apple.

Baxter, L. (1993). *The drawing book*. Nashville, TN: Hambleton–Hill.

Bradley, S. (1992). *How to draw cartoons*. Aspen, CO: Mad Hatter.

Butterfield, M. (1988). *How to draw machines.* Tulsa, OK: EDC.

David, M. (1993). *Cartooning for kids: A step–by–step guide to creating your own cartoons.* New York, NY: Harper Collins.

Dr. Seuss. (1987). *I can draw it myself: By me, myself with a little help from my friend Dr. Seuss.* New York, NY: Beginner.

Fleischman, P. (1993). *Copier creations: Using copy machines to make decals, silhouettes, flip books, films, and much more!* New York, NY: Harper Collins Children's Books.

Freeberg, E. & Freeberg D. (1987). *Simple graph art.* Westminster, CA: Teacher Created Material.

Heller, R. (1992). *Designs for coloring optical art.* New York, NY: Putnam Publication Group.

Lightfoot, M. (1993). *Cartooning for kids.* Buffalo, NY: Firefly Books Limited.

Tatchell, J. & Evans, C. (1987). *Young cartoonist.* Tulsa, OK: EDC.

Tollison, H. (1989). *Cartoon fun.* Tustin, CA: W Foster Publication.

Vaughan, G. & Jackson (1990). *Sketching drawing for children.* New York, NY: Putnam Publication Group.

WRITING

Artman, J. H. (1985). *The write stuff!* Carthage, IL: Good Apple.

Bauer, M. D. (1992). *What's your story? A young person's guide to writing fiction.* Boston, MA: Houghton Mifflin.

Broekel, R. (1986). *I can be an author.* Chicago, IL: Childrens.

Buhay, D. (1990). *Black and white of writing.* Allentown, PA: Hockenberry.

Cassedy, S. (1990). *In your own words: A beginner's guide to writing.* New York, NY: Harper Collins Childrens' Books.

Daniel, B. (1990). *Writing brainstorms.* Carthage, IL: Good Apple.

Fleisher, P. (1989). *Write now.* Carthage, IL: Good Apple.

Mammen, L. (1989). *Writing warm–ups.* ECS Learning Systems.

Ryan, E. (1992). *How to be a better writer.* Bronxville, NY: Troll Association.

Ryan, E. (1992). *How to write better book reports.* Bronxville, NY: Troll Association.

Stanish, B. (1983). *Creativity for kids through writing.* Cathage, IL: Good Apple.

Tchudi, S. & Tchudi, S. (1987). *The young writer's handbook: A practical guide for the beginner who is serious about writing.* New York, NY: Macmillan Childrens' Group.